21 DIFFICULT CONVERSATIONS

Tools to navigate your most important talk and master Exactly what to say.

21 DIFFICULT CONVERSATIONS

Tools to navigate your most important talk and master Exactly what to say.

By
Dr. Latha Vijaybaskar

Copyright © 2018 Dr. Latha Vijaybaskar

Publishing Services by Happy Self Publishing
www.happyselfpublishing.com

Year: 2018

All rights reserved. No reproduction, transmission or copy of this publication can be made without the written consent of the author in accordance with the provision of the Copyright Acts. Any person doing so will be liable to civil claims and criminal prosecution.

To my parents, for being my springboard—you made every leap of faith, safe.

To Vijay, my best half for being my sounding board— you have been with me through every step of this book, dream, and life.

To Shriram and Priyanka, for making me a dart board in every stimulating conversation—you both are my muse.

With the blessings of *Ganesha*, the elephant headed deity, whose tusk is said to have penned the lines below,

anudvega-karaṁ vākyaṁ satyaṁ priya-hitaṁ cayat
svādhyāyābhyasanaṁ caivavāṅ-mayaṁ tapa ucyate

BG.Ch:17.Stanza, 15.

Literal meaning: "Austerity of speech consists of speaking in a manner that will not agitate the minds of the listeners or enkindle the base emotions of the listener or his passion; the communication should be true. It must be beneficial to the listener and also pleasant. One should also engage in self study."

Table of Content

Foreword 9

Acknowledgments 13

Introduction 15

Conversation 1: The Most Difficult First Step 25

Conversation 2: Suspense Is For Thrillers Only 37

Conversation 3: The Dreaded NO 45

Conversation 4: Giving Feedback 51

Conversation 5: Arguments and Debates to Dialogues 59

Conversation 6: The Perfect Sorry 67

Conversation 7: How to Ask For A Raise and Other Such Conversations 75

Conversation 8: The Loquacious One 85

Conversation 9: Stay in The Game, Listen 93

Conversation 10: You Are What You Ask 101

Conversation 11: Emotional Outbursts, Temper, and Foul Language 109

Conversation 12: Delivering Bad News 117

Conversation 13: The Undiscussables—Responding To Personal Probes 123

Conversation 14: Ruminations—The Hurtful Mental Reruns 129

Conversation 15: The Chilling Silence 137

Conversation 16: The Art of Talk in the Digitally Distracted World 143

Conversation 17: Manager's Everyday Tough Talks 149

Conversation 18: Dealing the Blame Game 153

Conversation 19: Battle of Intentions and Influence 159

Conversation 20: Leadership Conversations 167

Conversation 21: The Outliers—When Conversations Are Not Enough 173

The Beginning! 179

Author Bio 181

Foreword

In my 24 years of work experience, I have seen that success in corporate and professional life depends on various leadership qualities. One such trait is how good a communicator you are. Apart from the clarity of thought and fluency of language, the one that that is most difficult and rare is the ability to be outspoken and direct.

Having a sit-down for a difficult conversation can be nerve-wracking. Many will find ways to totally avoid it. Unfortunately, challenging and difficult conversations are an unfortunate part of management. If you are a manager, you don't have a choice but to be good at it. If you are an entrepreneur or part of the senior management, it becomes even more important because, if the difficult situations are handled poorly, they can have implications on the morale of the employees and adversely impact staff retention.

This has a direct impact on the turnover of companies. A major study found that employees spend an average 3 hours a week dealing with conflict, which results in a net loss of US$350 billion in workforce costs.

The good news is that when these difficult conversations are handled properly, they can have a positive impact on employees' career and boost retention. There are very few people though who are natural at handling these conversations. These are people who are willing to face the tough situations head-on and engage in difficult conversations while most others pussyfoot around or worse, avoid completely.

It's interesting to note that it is people with these qualities that are respected the most within an organization and consequently, they are the ones who are fastest to climb the corporate ladder. Clearly, there is a strong correlation between having the ability to have difficult conversations and corporate success.

I have known Dr Latha Vijaybaskar on a professional capacity as a fellow core committee member of the Professional Speakers Association of India. I have seen her put these strategies in action during many discussions. Her insights come from her practical experience. I love the fact that she has distilled the essence of difficult conversation from experts such as Mark Goulsten, William Ury and insights from Harvard Negotiation Project.

Latha is a natural storyteller and she has peppered the chapters with stories that you can easily relate. I would highly recommend reading this book and one should treat this as an important investment in their personal career growth.

Kiruba Shankar
President, Professional Speakers Association of India
CEO, Breathe Digital

Acknowledgments

21 Difficult Conversations is a journey and many have traveled this path with me. The very first in this journey is my best half, Vijaybaskar, who has pushed me to achieve all that I dreamt of. He has played the tough dual role of being my fan and an immense critic, balancing the insanity with grace and wit.

This book, right from its inception, has been a collective query of many, and it is those participants, executives, students, and leaders of my sessions that I would like to thank for bringing this book to life. If not for you, these conversations would have been wrapped up at the end of a training session.

From thoughts to words was difficult but the journey from draft to published copy is a writer's nightmare. If not for Jyotsna Ramachandran, of Happy Self Publishing and her encouragement, I may not have dared to show this draft outside. Her team lead by Sushmitha Naroor has lovingly crafted every sentence of this book with me. Thank you, team, you made this journey a lot less arduous than it should have been and thanks for putting up with me patiently when I missed yet another deadline. I would also like to thank my editor Radhika Pillai from Happy Self Publishing.

The book looks catchy thanks to the team of the designer- Rac from Happy Self Publishing who worked on a number of my ideas and actually listened every time.

Seeing your words in print can be scary but for a lifetime of love, encouragement, and support from my parents.

My muse to writing a good copy have been my two kids, Priyanka (Thank you for the book promo videos, website updates and generally all things technical that I never seem to understand) and Shriram (for reading every chapter and encouraging me) my nephew Rishi and niece Nisha who have helped with their enthusiasm in deciding the cover designs.Lastly, as I have always said, I am first a bookworm. Everything that I have learned stems from my passion for the written word, and I would like to thank my uncle P.V.Gopalakrishnan for introducing me to the magical realm of reading.

And now, thank you, reader! By reading this book and every time you brave yourself to have a difficult conversation, - you make my vision come true.

Introduction

In the days before I married my Kindle, my usual haunts were the city's bookstores. During one such trip, I was looking for a particular book for my doctoral thesis on internal corporate communication and engagement. Of course, I was not expecting a hundred copies of the book, as I know how niche the segment of my research is. In fact, I did not find a single copy of the book.

A young and eager store staff member approached me, a hesitant smile pasted on his face, for the sake of customer care.

"May I help you?" he asked.

My smile of relief and the yes I said, was heartfelt. I asked him to look for the book I wanted and I met with a blank stare.

"Err what is it about?" I am sure he was not interested in the book; and for want of a simpler description, I said "Communications."

"Oh! That's great. Please follow me." My Aladdin started walking rapidly toward a long aisle, with me trotting a this heels happily.

He stopped at this huge aisle full of books and started searching. After a tense five minutes, I dared to voice my doubt—"Why are you searching for my book in the Technology section?"

He looked at me and said, "You wanted a book on communication, isn't it?"

I was lost for a moment and then it dawned upon me. I laughed and said, "I did not mean machines communicating. I mean people talking to each other?"

He looked at me, "You may want to try the self-help section."

Very true, young man. Today in the age of computers, social media, phones, and text messages, the human element of communicating is delegated to the self-help and psychology section. Moreover, to ensure that this book stays with the human touch, it is named *conversations*—difficult, emotional, and uncertain.

What is a difficult conversation?

Let us dig right in with the sentence we least want to hear—We need to talk.

It is the single most squirm-inducing phrase in any conversation—one that no one really wants to hear. We all have conversations that we dread to talk and hear about. It can be asking for a raise or even terminating an employment. It can be saying no or asking for a yes. Giving critical feedback or confronting someone. Maybe apologizing.

At work, home, commute with friends, coworkers and enemies alike, a difficult conversation is one where you feel uncomfortable and the stakes are high.

These can consist of conversations that you feel deeply about, or are vulnerable to, when the outcomes are uncertain and are potential grounds for making every word bleed. Even general topics like sexuality, race, politics, and religion are difficult topics to discuss.

We are in this dilemma often. Do we confront or avoid it? Should we speak our opinion on the political situation today or leave it to the editorial pages to fill in?

Does being diplomatic work? Let me share a personal experience.

Why are some conversations difficult?

An acquaintance of mine loves her mobile. It's even better if it is her voice that she hears. A unique ability to speak for a few hours without a topic or any direction is one of her specialties. Over time, she had become a very good friend and I did not want to hurt her. Most of the time I plug in my earphones and continue my work, as the monologue continues. An occasional yes, ah, and a few grunts are encouragement enough for her.

During one such call many years back, when my acumen for dealing with a difficult conversation was not as it is today, I decided to ask my husband for help and made him call my name out loudly so that she could hear. I made these urgent phrases up in my mind to apologize and cut that call. What she said next was priceless.

"Please ask him what he wants. What we are speaking is important. As an independent, empowered woman you should not reply to loud summons."

I learnt the three most important lessons in conversation that day.

1. The purpose of the conversation is in its response.
2. Do unto others what you want others to do to you; may not work always.

3. There is no diplomatic way to throw a bomb.

In my attempt to end the conversation above, we were two separate islands. We might as well have been speaking different languages. In one of my training sessions for a sales team, a participant wanted to know how to get the customers to see his point of view. And that is where we make mistakes.

A complaining customer is angry, feels he or she is right, and expects an apology. An employee is oftentimes more worried about how to solve the issue quickly and whether it might affect his job or target.

These two islands talk across the table without satisfaction. They are talking like my friend and I did, but there was no actual communication.

> **Not all conversations are communication and unless everyone is on the same page, there will be no effective outcome.**

People talk and listen only to the information that they want. Perceptual bias is a writhing, thriving element of any tense conversation. You have all faced these tense situations.

- Your organization prides itself on being flat. There are only open seating and glass cabins. Yet, you have not confronted your boss on your views on the last project.

- You speak daily, meet frequently and work a few feet away from each other, but find it difficult to work as a team.

In any tense situation, we try to solve it, the way we would look at the problem. The reason why a situation is difficult lays on the very foundation that people are on different pages. Therefore trying to solve the issue from your viewpoint may not work.

In my conversation example, I assumed that my friend would apologize (as I might have done) and cut the call as I clearly had work elsewhere. Unfortunately, the importance she gave to the conversation was a lot more than what I did. What was a mildly irritating conversation for me was probably an emotionally satisfying one for her.

It is in this unclear path that we chart our relationships and wonder if we should keep quiet or raise our concern. Tact is good. Softening the blow is a tactic often advised, but let us understand that there if no soft way to fire your colleague or in my case to tell my friend that she drives me crazy. As Stone, Patton, and Heen mention in their book, *Difficult Conversations*, there is no diplomatic way to throw a hand grenade. However much you try to cushion its fall, it will bring destruction in its wake. The alternative is to silently sit on the ticking bomb and that would be detrimental to you; and it would burst at some inopportune moment.

So easy advises like be tactful and stay positive are too superfluous, and the issue runs far deeper than just mere words.

What is this book about?

This book has a single goal—to fiercely bring to light those difficult conversations that are central to your success and to show exactly what to say.

As I mentioned earlier, vague solutions like stay patient, or be positive, serves no purpose in a difficult and messy conversation.

In fact, every conversation turns difficult due to different reasons.

This book prepares you for twenty-one of those known eventualities and provides tactical insights to each conversation.

How did I distil down these particular twenty-one conversations?

I asked people.

In my classes and workshops, I often ask what is that one conversation that they are very uncomfortable having. This book is the collective query of many and the top twenty-one among them have been discussed, analyzed, and solved.

From *where do I start talking* to *how do I make someone stop speaking*; *from saying no, giving feedback, delivering bad news, turning debates to dialogues, to going back to an old hurtful incident;* you will find life affirming primers to have those conversations you need to have the most.

This book heavily draws support and guidance from great works and theories on communication and human behavior.

From Socrates' questioning to Aristotle's thoughts, from the celebrated Harvard negotiation project to Ury's theories to Mark Goulsten's remarkable insights on human behavior, each conversation is enhanced with situations and solutions.

Along with the theories, I will support you chapter by chapter by telling you stories and situations that you can connect with, helping you understand and learn exactly what to say.

How to use this book?

Just open page one and keep reading until you reach the end. Please remember to donate this book at the end to someone who will really use it.

I seriously think the book should have a disclaimer—not for light reading.

On a serious note, you can either follow the chapters as is, and read each of the twenty-one difficult conversations in the order it is written, to understand how every difficult conversation can be answered. But if you are like me and have a set of conversations that became difficult during your experience, then please feel free to follow the *"necessity is the mother of invention"* method and jump to the conversation that you have difficulty with at the moment and later work on the others.

Each chapter is a stand-alone single difficult conversation.

My advice is to have some pen and paper with you while you read. Create your own examples or reflect on the difficult conversations you have had. Once that is done, write down exactly what you would say based on your learning from the chapter.

Then make the life-transforming decision to try them out in life.

It is vital that you start practicing what you read immediately as 'one of these days' will mostly translate itself to 'none of these days.'

And I should know this. As a bookworm, my usual solution to any problem is to read about it. I have internalized books on yoga, strength training, even pilates and yet the stubborn arrow on the weighing machine refuses to move left.

As the French say—it's the first step that costs.

Let's begin!

CONVERSATION 1

THE MOST DIFFICULT FIRST STEP

Mrs. Higgins: But you mustn't. I'm serious, Henry. You offend all my friends: they stop coming whenever they meet you.

Higgins: Nonsense! I know I have no small talk; but people don't mind.

Mrs. Higgins: Oh! Don't they? Small talk indeed! What about your large talk? Really, dear, you mustn't stay.

**'Pygmalion' Act III Sc 1.
George Bernard Shaw**

It is the most important meeting of your career. A make or break deal, with the client and you have spent the last few weeks working insane hours for it. You are pumped for the meeting; you arrive early at the client's office after a sleepless night, tossing your anxious self around. You walk inside the office with a smile, shake hands, and what are the first few words you speak to him?

Most people will spend all their energy, blood, and sweat on the finer points of the meeting. The offers, arguments, negotiation points, research, competition, and pricing will take the focus. But only a few will actually come prepared to ease the client into the conversation.

Conversations are like moving through a maze. Different routes will lead to very different paths and choosing the right beginning may set the tone for a smoother and less dangerous journey.

In my many training programs, I have often made the above question *situation with the client* into a game and asked participants what their first sentence would be?

The most shocking answer I have received yet has been—"I will give you a discount" as the opening sentence.

It's awkward when people leapfrog up the ladder of communication. If you want to climb the ladder of success, you need to climb the ladder of communication, starting at the bottom rung: **small talk.**

Small talk is how you could easily start a conversation. But what to start talking about is the difficult part of the conversation.

Why is small talk difficult?

When we were children, we have been taught—not to talk to strangers. Growing up, whenever a stranger meets us, our inborn Darwinian survival skills spring up and we look for a place to run.

It can be a meeting, a business-networking event, or even an interview. That twinge of nervousness, the feeling you may be called a bore or not interesting, keeps you from even greeting the other person. Such anxiety would make even a party hall an obstacle course.

By the end of the day, you'll end up thinking, 'What if I had talked to that person?' after spending the entire evening nursing varied sentences that you never spoke.

Ninety-nine percent of all new relationships begin with small talk. You unconsciously indulge in small talk all the time. For example, you routinely meet people on your morning jog, at the grocery store, while dropping the kids at school, events, even in the elevator and during these periods, you often behave on autopilot. The autopilot conversation goes something like this -

I. *Blank stare.*
II. *Hi.*
III. *Hi.*
IV. *How are you?*
V. *Good. And you?*
VI. *Good.*
VII. *Shuffle. Look elsewhere. Move away.*

Then you go on with your day, never really making a genuine connection.

The words "*Hi! How are you?*" is an invitation. They open doors to a thousand conversations and yet it is only used to fill awkward silences.

The beauty of a small talk is that it stimulates a wide range of emotions, opening minds and hearts and brings deeper, meaningful relationships.

Most people will talk well when they feel confident and trust the audience. In a situation where you meet new people and trust is yet to be built, anxiety often shadows confidence.

The Effective Small Talk

In a study conducted on 44 supervisors by David Moutoux and Micheal Porter at the University of Cincinnati, they concluded that small talk has a positive influence on the employee turnover, absenteeism, production, and efficiency.

Starting a conversation is very important and most importantly, what you say need not be something clever or dripping in complexity. Simple comments, observations, and questions work wonders.

> **When it comes to small talk, you have only one simple rule:**
> **Don't aim for brilliant; aim for pleasant.**

That makes it easier for the other person to open up. Small talk is like a trailer to a movie. The good ones create enough curiosity to make you pay to watch the entire movie.

That said these are the three things to master in the small talk challenge.

1. Master your introduction
Many great conversations are around a common point of interest and if you can offer it during your introduction, an opening on what interests you; that can make a great conversation starter. Now you have a door wide open to build rapport. If you can add humor here, that acts like a catalyst.

Everyone appreciates a good laugh and it will quickly expand your group. Although there is nothing like a perfect opener, you will have a simple mix and match pattern of three topics and three ways to start those topics.

You can either talk about the current situation, i.e. the environment of the meeting, the other person, or yourself.

And then you can ask a question, state a fact, or voice your opinion.

➢ *Stating facts*
The most common and ineffective way to begin a conversation is by stating facts about you. I often hear opening sentences like,

"Hi, I am Ravi. I work at ABC international."

By reciting facts, the other person is not involved in the conversation and the best you will get is a polite smile or a few filler words like great, that's good, etc. Some good souls try to ask more about what you do and are fed with more facts.

"I work in marketing."

Reciting facts about a situation like "the traffic was maddening today" is also ineffective as it does not involve the other person in the conversation.

➢ *Voicing opinion*
Opinions are a much better way to start a conversation. Many people love nothing more than a good, hard argument, even if the subject was trivial and their points weak.

The only glitch in the situation is that it is rather difficult to open a sentence to a stranger by saying, "I think the plastic ban is yet another thoughtless thing by the current government. They just impulsively issue some order or the other." This was a true sentence in one of my WhatsApp groups one morning. An immediate reply that came was, "This was piloted in Bangalore in my locality three years ago and has been brought to the rest of the city for almost two years now. So it certainly was not impulsive."

Yes, it ensured a lot of talk that day but this is like living on the edge. You may tumble into the dark lands of ego and argument.

Do not consider opening sentences that offer opinions about the other person. That will be rude. Opinions about you as an opening sentence will be narcissistic.

> *Asking a good question*

By far a thoughtful question is the best invitation for a conversation. It is easier to start the conversation with "I see you have come prepared with a beautiful jute bag. How are you feeling about the plastic ban?"

This question is about the other person's viewpoint and captures the current situation well, displaying an open attitude.

After you have asked the question, make sure to listen carefully to understand your audience.

2. Master listening skills
Listen with your eyes and ears. Listen to what is said and pay more attention to the things left unsaid. Build empathy toward your speaker and be genuinely interested in what they say. Listening is not waiting for your chance to speak. It is encouraging the other person to build a strong relation based on trust, with you. Channel your natural curiosity into small talk.

More on listening is discussed in chapter nine.

3. Master the conversation past the pleasantries
The very idea of a small talk is to pave a way for a deeper relationship. If they end every day like the conversation my two neighbors have, it is pointless.

Neighbor 1: Good morning.
Neighbor 2: Good morning.
Neighbor 1: Going for your walk?
Neighbor 1: Yes I am.
Neighbor 1: Ok
Neighbor 1: Ok.

How do we continue the conversation while keeping it interesting and flowing? How do we make sure there are no awkward silences, small talk that doesn't move on to the real conversation? The previous mastery comes to our rescue here. Listen keenly and respond with zeal to drive the conversation past the small talk to deeper ones on interests, passions, opinions, and philosophy. Show your vulnerable side. This will build trust and make the other person open up too. Build on the commonalities to create flourishing friendships. Many business ventures begin while running a marathon, playing golf, or even lifting weights.

Master these three to have a meaningful conversation with just about anyone.

Exactly what to say

<u>Somewhere on the office floors.</u>

Person 1: Hi
Person 2: Hi there. I haven't seen you before. Have you joined recently?

Person 1: I've been here for three weeks now. I work in marketing.
Person 2: Oh man! Lucky you. You get paid more and don't have to listen to the complaints. I work in customer care.

<u>*(It is inappropriate to talk money in small talk. Also, avoid whining.)*</u>

Person 1: Sounds interesting to me. Your ears are always on the ground. So tell me, how do the customers like our new campaign?

Person 2: It's ok. Hey, do you want to go out for coffee?

(He has left a clear opening about the new campaign slide by. And jumped the ladder to go out for coffee. The listener will walk away.)

Person 1: Not really. I should be getting back to work.
Person 2: Yeah, me too. At least tomorrow is a weekend. What are your plans tomorrow?

(Too early after the failed coffee offer.)

Person 1: Vegetate in front of the TV, I guess.
Person 2: Of course! We have India vs. Sri Lanka. Who do you think will win?

Person 1: I am not really a sports fan
Person 2: Oh! It's going to be a great game. You must watch it.

(It is inappropriate to continue a topic the other person is not interested in.)

Person 1: I will try. Bye
Person 2: Bye.

Now let's try again.

Somewhere on the office floors.

Person 1: Hi
Person 2: Hi there. I haven't seen you before. Have you joined recently?

Person 1: I've been here for three weeks now. I work in marketing.
Person 2: That's wonderful. We work in complement roles. I work in customer care.

Person 1: Sounds interesting to me. Your ears are always on the ground. So tell me, how do the customers like our new campaign?
Person 2: I am getting mixed views right now. Guess it is just early days. This weekend reviews will give us more insights.

Person 1: Yes. I am waiting for that as well. I should be getting back to work.
Person 2: Yeah, me too. At least tomorrow is a weekend. What are your plans tomorrow?

Person 1: Vegetate in front of the TV, I guess. What are your plans?
Person 2: I am a cricket fan. There is a match on TV. What are your hobbies?

Person 1: I am not really a sports fan. I am more a people person.

Person 2: Say, do you want to go to the club? We have a huge crowd watching on that life-sized screen with great food?

Person 1: Sounds good. I'll meet you tomorrow.
Person 2: See you tomorrow then.

Conversation 2

Suspense Is For Thrillers Only

"Any conversation which does not include the context of the journey of the heart is by definition untrue to who we are as human beings."

Marianne Williamson

One of the most common reasons for the lack of trust in a relationship, is people don't know where they stand. An employee at my program said—"I am all right with a harsh feedback but I want to know what the fallouts are."

"Meet me in my office at 5:00 p.m." is the most ominous message you can receive from your boss. Imagine when this message is sent at 9:00 a.m., the whole day is ruined thinking about the 5:00 p.m. meeting.

As you enter the room after a whole day of wondering why you are here your manager asks you "So what's been happening in your team?" *(The ineffectiveness of this question is dealt with in the **You are what you ask** chapter.)*

You don't know which one of the thousand issues is on the table today. You smile and say tensely "Things are good."

After a lot of back and forth talk, your manager finally speaks about the issue at hand.

This kind of surprise builds distrust in a relationship. Think about how simple it would have been if the manager had initially sent a message—meet me at 5:00 p.m. to discuss (this) issue.

You will be prepared and willing to solve the problem in hand, rather than wonder what the issue itself was. More importantly, you know where you stand.

In any serious conversation, the receiver needs to know what will happen now.

> **It is the suspense that makes a conversation difficult not the issue.**

The more the conversation is going to mean to you, the more important it is for your conversation partner to understand the big picture.

If you need to have a long, complex, or emotion-laden conversation with someone, it will make a big difference if you briefly explain your conversational intention first and then invite the consent of your intended conversation partner.

As a manager if you can set the context at the outset "I have called to tell you that the last month's results are not really good and we need to work on a strategy to make it better this month" the team member will receive this talk positively. He knows where he stands.

Why is this difficult?

1. We work from the assumption that others can see and feel what we ourselves do. While in reality, they work from their viewpoint.

According to William Jennings Bryan, "Two people in a conversation amounts to four people talking. The four are what one person says, what he really wanted to say, what the listener heard, and what he thought he heard." The words we speak, the words we hear, the words we mean, and the words that get understood are all different.

Alfred Korzybski has coined a great phrase for the differing assumptions, "the map is not the territory." The idea seems simple enough—who, after all, would confuse a roadmap with a road, or a menu with a meal?

Yet Korzybski observed that people would often confuse what they think with 'reality.' It is clear that people perceive reality as the place from which they talk, and it might be received from a completely different reality.

In my personal experience, I had received a similar—meet me at 5:00 p.m. message. From my reality, the client meant a lot to my growth and I had put in a lot of work into my training. I was very anxious for the meeting. After a tense morning, I realized that I was called to be congratulated on some great participant feedback. Looking back, I could see that there was nothing threatening in the message, yet I was anxious. A lack of setting context makes a conversation difficult because our fear changes our reality.

> **Our fear changes our reality. We interpret and understand differently under anxiety and fear.**

2. Anxiety and fear changes how we interpret what is being conveyed and, therefore, we can work on different realities.

Think back to the most emotional conversation you have had recently at work and at home. What are the chances that the conversation ended badly with each person feeling like the other person was misunderstood?

You got angry because they assumed the worst while you were trying to be at your best. You can avoid this type of drama by starting potentially difficult conversations, by stating your intention.

3. The iceberg effect throws dangerous undercurrents.

In 1930, Ernest Hemingway claimed that an author does not have to explicitly reveal the deeper meaning of a story. We all remember his six-word story. Every writer and moviemaker works on this basic premise of 'show and not tell' to build suspense. While it is a great way to read what happens to the protagonist in a three hundred-page crime thriller, it is hardly the right way to talk, in real life.

Like the iceberg, only 10 percent of the conversation is visible and the rest of it consists of body language and the receiver's interpretation. To lower this waterline, clear context and an invitation to respond from the receiver is necessary.

> **Like Richard Ford says,
> "Fear and Hope are alike underneath."**

This is especially true while reprimanding a child. Children are a lot more imaginative than adults are, and can take every word literally and weave stories in their minds. Avoid asking, "Do you know what you have done?" and allow fear and anxiety to hang there.

Tell them. Reprimand them. You could even punish. However, don't let the suspense ruin the relation.

Exactly what to say

You can avoid the dramatic responses by starting potentially difficult conversations by stating your intention.

To a team member
Instead of saying -
"We need to talk about your project timelines. Meet me later."
Try saying -
"I see some of the deadlines on your project have slipped. Can we meet in the evening to discuss a workable schedule to map them back on track?"

To your teenage son -
Instead of saying -
"What have you been doing all day?"
Try saying -

"What are your plans for this holiday? Is there something new you want to try?"

<u>To your wife -</u>
Instead of saying -
"You bought yet another bag?"
Try saying -
"I want to save for our holiday and I find that we keep running short of money due to impulsive purchases. Can we work on a better plan?"

<u>To your boss -</u>
Instead of saying -
"I want to move out of the project."
Try saying -
"There are five major projects currently being handled and I have more experience in *this* one. Can we speak more about my ideas over lunch today?"

Conversation 3

The Dreaded NO

NO. It is not a word, but a complete sentence in itself.

It does not require the crutch of explanation or context.

No, simply means no.

A translated dialogue from the Hindi movie Pink

One of the most powerful dialogues in a recent movie titled *Pink*, the rich baritone of Amitabh Bachhan's voice as he delivers the dialogue toward the courtroom in the climax of the movie; must have moved every audience member. And rightly so, as the movie fights sexual harassment.

In reality, however, you fight everyday in your lives, homes, work, and community to say **no**. The pressure to give in and say yes in today's stress-ridden, over-choiced world is limitless.

On any average day, do you face a request or a demand that is unwelcome?

Are you at the receiving end of an inappropriate behavior?

Did you feel like a situation or a system is not working well or fair?

It can be overwork, doing favors, or social obligations; because we are socially designed to be people pleasers, it is notoriously difficult for us say a simple no.

Let me give you an example.

Imagine you are planning a great weekend trip with your family. You have informed your boss about your plans, booked your tickets, and are excitedly counting down to Friday to spend the evening with your four-year-old. Suddenly you get a call from your boss asking you to join your team on a project, through the weekend. What would you do?

    A. Grudgingly say yes, disappointing your family and go to work.

B. Remind your boss that you have already asked for the weekend off and cannot change.
C. Do not pick up any calls from the boss.

If you have chosen any of the above options, you *need* to learn how to say NO.

The first option was to say yes—accommodate and sacrifice your key interests. While you may feel like the decision is important to your job, you have actually said no to another important part of your life.

The second option was to say a poor version of no that might affect the long-term relationship you share with your boss. Such a no is observed as an attack and therefore becomes abrasive and detrimental to relationships.

The third is avoidance—a hope that the problem will vanish away. Such tactics of snuggling under a blanket should have been weaned off in your adolescence.

None of the options is a win-win situation.

And therein lays the problem. We are forever choosing between saying yes to have harmony, and saying no in order to protect our interests.

Maybe if we could learn to say no and still leave the door open, the no wouldn't be so bad. All too often, our greatest obstacle is our inability to say no without offending.

How does one not fall into the trap of *attack, accommodate, and avoid* and say the great NO?

How to say a positive no?

William Ury, in his book *The Power of a Positive No* teaches us how to say a positive no and still get to the yes. Whether it is to a customer or a coworker, a client or the CEO, his *no* is cleverly sandwiched between two yeses and it creates a positive impact.

> **Ury believes that, "Yes without No is appeasement, whereas No without Yes is war."**

Therefore, his positive *no* starts with a yes and ends with a yes. In his words, "For Yes is the key word of community, No is the key word of individuality. Yes is the key word of connection, No is the key word of protection. Yes is the key word of peace, No is the key word of justice."

To consider Ury's theory in our example above,

YES: *Thanks Sid (boss) for the opportunity to be a part of the project. However as you know I had applied for leave this weekend, as it is very* *important to me to be with my family at this point in time.*

NO: *Therefore, I will be unable to come during this weekend for the project work.*

YES: *I will however come early on Monday to continue with the project, and I can ensure that the deadlines will be completed on time.*

This method of saying no allows the listener to know the reason for your no. It is a larger yes that you want and the boss is pacified that the targets will not be affected, thus this creates lesser friction.

Ury's theory is one of the most celebrated ones in a negotiation. It directly corroborates with Daniel Kahneman's *Peak-End* theory. This says that, when looking back, people do not necessarily recall their feelings throughout an experience. Instead, they remember the way they felt at:

- *The peak times—the intense times—in the experience.*
- *The end of the experience.*

The peak times may be pleasant or unpleasant. These are the memories that stay with us; as does the way we felt at the end of the experience.

While using this theory to say **no**, the listener is going to remember the no—as well as the peak and how the conversation ends. Using Ury's positive No, the end will always be positive, making way for a better relationship at the end of the no.

Exactly what to say

You are asked to volunteer (yet again) for your neighborhood project

"I am flattered that you want me to volunteer but I am not in a position to accept the post this year. However, next year, I hope the circumstances will change and I can volunteer again."

Your supervisor asks you to do an extra project.

"I feel proud that you chose me for this project, but I am already tied down with three running projects. Would you like me to reprioritize?"

You are asked to be the speaker of another non-paid event where you do not stand to gain anything.

"I really appreciate you asking me to speak. However, my calendar is already busy that day, may I recommend someone else?

(Or) I will help promote the event in my blog and social media."

Conversation 4

Giving Feedback

"To become more effective and fulfilled at work, people need a keen understanding of their impact on others and the extent to which they're achieving their goals in their working relationships. Direct feedback is the most efficient way for them to gather this information and learn from it."

Ed Batista

In the early days of my career, I worked in the Human Resources department and performance appraisal period was my least favorite time of the year. As a fresher right out of college, I did not have to write appraisals but I had to ensure that all senior managers have completed their appraisals for their teams. I used to feel like a dentist extracting a particularly stubborn tooth. One manager even went to say, "I will do the appraisals after the targets are met, as the employee morale comes down for weeks after the appraisal and I don't have the time to babysit right now."

Feedback should not be a cringe-inducing difficult conversation, right? Wrong. Most people hate feedback. Both giving and receiving it.

Why is giving feedback so difficult?

Why is it difficult to tell our teams, our employees (even our spouse or friends) that something is not right and that things need to change?

1. The defensive reaction is scary
We are worried of what the reaction might be. What if he or she gets angry? What if they cry and shout? What if they go on and on about why they are right and you are wrong? What if they take it personally?

Well, they are supposed to take it personally.

Feedback is personal, and a defensive reaction is to be expected. It is what makes us human. These defensive reactions make people ride the feedback journey from the sidelines, brushing just around the edges and never entering into the deep waters.

While you are wondering about how to react, the feedback ends up being vague and may sound false.

The tendency to begin positively does not cushion the blow, it makes the whole thing distinctly patronizing. For example,

"You did a great job on the project, but..."

From the listener's viewpoint he is hearing, *"You are such a good team member but your reports are not good."* And he thinks, *If my reports are not good, how am I a good team member?*

This kind of feedback is confusing. The *but* negates anything positive before it. In fact, this positive patronizing opening has become so common that people begin to cringe on hearing anything positive, expecting a 'but'.

If feedback needs to be given, it should be done quickly. No one wants to hear about how he or she failed for twenty minutes.

2. Feedback should not be reserved only for the negative

The next reason why feedback is so difficult is because most people focus only on the negative feedback. Giving an authentic positive feedback is equally hard.

"Great job Avyay. You are a great asset to the team."
This is a sweet but useless feedback.

As with constructive feedback, positive feedback should also be specific and help the receiver try to understand what to replicate.

You could try to be specific and say *"Great job Avyay. I really appreciate that you put in extra research to understand the client requirement and you have delivered without affecting the cost."*

According to Shari Harley, keynote speaker, coach, and CEO of Candid Culture, there are only two reasons to give feedback—***to encourage someone to either change or replicate a behavior.***

All other feedback is not feedback. They may be opinions, comments, or judgments.

The effective feedback process

> **Successful feedback brings the conversation to focus on actions and behaviors.**

The right feedback time and place

The annual performance review is not the time to dust out past performance discussions. They will not bring forth any new change. For feedback, it is always better to strike the iron when it is hot.

Feedback should be provided as soon as the event is done. Try to approach it within a day or positively within the week.

The location is very important too. Feedback should be provided face to face. A telephonic conversation or an email is easy but it will not bring about the desired change in a person. It is also important to find a place where people cannot hear you deliver the constructive feedback. Therefore, it has to be a private cabin in the office, and not the open cubicle.

The pre-feedback process

Feedback is an important business. Pay a little attention to get it right, and you will see a changed team member. Before you begin your feedback conversation, keep the following ready:

1. Write down what you plan to say
2. Write down the incidents or actions clearly and accurately, to avoid any miscommunication. Now read them and remove all words that sound judgmental.
3. Look for a solution and what should change.

The feedback itself

The following seven steps will ensure that every feedback is effective and that the receiver works toward the change. Inspired by Shari Harley's eight-point pattern, these are a few steps to follow:

Step 1: Set the stage
Ask for permission to give feedback, set the stage on what you want to talk about, and establish the context right. People will thank you when they know what to expect from the conversation.

Step 2: Describe the example
This is the behavior that you have observed, for which you are giving the feedback. Being specific and recent will allow your receiver to relate objectively.

Step 3: Specify the effect of behavior
Share what the consequence of his or her behavior is and how it impacts the organization or the team. Be specific.

Step 4: Initiate the Change
Make a suggestion or provide alternatives. Allow discussion at this stage. Ask questions, listen, and empathize. Encourage the person to develop an action plan.

Step 5: Build the commitment
Establish the next steps, a plan for the change, and how it will be measured. These steps require total commitment from the receiver and thus making it a dialogue.

Step 6: Thank your participant
Say thank you to close the feedback and show your appreciation for the positive response.

Exactly what to say

A sample performance feedback

Step 1:
Ravi, I need to speak with you. Can you meet me in my office for ten minutes? We need to discuss yesterday's sales promotion event.

Step 2:
Ravi, I am sorry to say but I have noticed that the sales promotion event did not go as planned. I have noticed errors in the execution and delay from the supply chain.

Step 3:
As a result, we have not achieved the sales target that we set out to achieve in the planning stage. As the person in charge of the project, what are your thoughts on yesterday's event?

Step 4:
Listen. Have a dialogue. Understand their viewpoint.

Step 5:
Your points are valid. So here is my request. As you mentioned we will quickly rework the vendor management. Moving forward, I would like to know

about the issues when they occur so that we can act immediately. Can we meet every Thursday at 5:00 p.m. until the end of the sales promotion?

Step 6:

Thank you, Ravi for speaking with an open mind. I look forward to completing this project successfully.

Conversation 5

Arguments and Debates to Dialogues

"Certain ways of communicating alienate us from our natural state of compassion."

Marshall B. Rosenberg

Freedom of speech, balance of opinions, listening to both sides' debates, arguments. Who can question these constructive tools in conversation?

A quick look at your social media feed, the television or even a glance at today's headlines will show you a completely different picture. The words that are used are not collaborative. They are downright abrasive, like we are at war.

Some of the headlines on my current feed -

- Lousy economics and lousier politics
- Government endangering our security infrastructure
- Largest U.S. business group attacks Trump on tariffs
- WhatsApp becomes India's new serial killer.

Today the best way to cover news is to express the most extreme and polarized view. The best way to win a situation is to pit against the other party.

We are moving toward a society where arguments, debates, and **my** views are so important that every discussion has become a debate. Every discussion uses an argumentative language.

It is not just the news and media, but Facebook too (on women's day for inclusion of more women in the workplace) that shows feeds that read, "battle of the sexes" or "breaking the glass ceiling."

TV shows are named the kitchen wars, the melody war, the battle to its bitter end. Today schools have contests called the dance wars, the war room, marketing warfare, etc.

Where are we heading with these battle-laden minds? Words like annihilation are commonly used by schoolchildren to convey simple things like "I'll beat you in a game."

Words are the ideas upon which change is built. Language invisibly molds our way of thinking about events, people, and concepts around us.

> Deborah Tannen in her book *The Argumentative Culture* says—"taking a warlike stance in contexts that are not literally war—pervades our public and private discourse, leading us to approach issues and each other in an adversarial spirit. The resulting *argument culture* makes it more difficult to solve problems and is corrosive to the human spirit."

How we speak during times of conflict, decides how the conflict will be resolved. Speaking in war-like terms in a non-combat situation is dangerous.

The common man's argument

It is in this argument culture that we live, thrive, and work every day. We are criticized, appraised, and judged in the same way.

No matter how good your relationships are or how much of an expert you are in your field, there are two things to be remembered:

- You are not always right
- You will be criticized at some point.

Debating has its merits in winning or proving ourselves right but moving toward a dialogue, is to learn to speak without polarizing issues, invalidating or hurting others, and taking responsibility of our actions.

Deborah L. Flick, Ph.D. in her book *From Debate to Dialogue: Using the Understanding Process to Transform Our Conversations* says—"Unfortunately we are so steeped in debate, proving one's point and challenging others, that alternative possibilities for interaction are often eclipsed from our view. It is interesting to notice that even when we say we want to dialogue we commonly end up in debate."

The problem with debate is its premise, which conveys that the views are opposing. Debate, however, powerful is a strategy advocating a particular polarized, fixed position. Debate is the language for maintaining a status quo and creating a verbal battlefield.

For stronger communities, healthier relationships and vibrant organizations, it is necessary to move toward dialogues that promote progress and nurtures trust. Dialogue does not mean losing our stand. We do not need to change our views, but our attitude. It is possible to continue disagreeing without demonizing others. It is also possible to continue disagreeing about some issues while working together on others.

Why is dialogue difficult?

Consider any conversation in your recent memory. What are the chances that they were opinionated, judgmental, or defensive?

Consider a very common and mundane line -

Person 1: You were supposed to call me yesterday.

Depending on the nature of our relation with the person, our debating mind that hates to lose, rushes in defense and chooses any one of the following four options-

1. *Excuse*—"Oh! I am so sorry. My battery ran out and I had such a bad time with the rain and traffic. It was a miracle that I reached home safe."
2. *Attack*—"So now we are keeping tabs are we? You could just as well have picked up your phone and called me. Had you done that you'd have realized what a busy day I had."
3. *Denial*—"Really? As I remember it, you were supposed to call me. I waited a good couple of hours for your call. I never forget my responsibilities."
4. *Avoidance*—"Please let's not start an argument. Tell me what you wanted or else let's catch up tomorrow."

These typically defensive responses arise from the argumentative mentality of not disturbing our position.

Marshall Rosenberg in his book on nonviolent communication uses the term *life alienating communication*. This life alienating communication can be compared to the *language of the jackal* that judges, criticizes, appraises, and threatens.

According to Rosenberg, these kinds of communications are actually personal desires in disguise.

On the other hand, the *language of the giraffe* is the language of requests that allows us to communicate with others in a respectful and compassionate way. Giraffes have the largest hearts of all land animals (up to forty lbs!) Jackals, due to their low proximity to the ground, tend to see what is just under their noses. Jackal language symbolizes characteristics of shortsightedness, self-protection, and limited communication.

Look back into your recent arguments. What kind of defenses do you generally rely on?

Exactly what to say

The following four-step process can turn every debate into a dialogue, every criticism into an opportunity.

1. *Ask for details*—To discuss from all sides, it is imperative to know the arguments of the other side. By asking for details, you are minimizing the potential of a fight. You are also giving a chance to your opponent to present his case without censure.
2. *Listen to understand*—As you ask for details; do not mentally stack up points for an argument. Listen to understand.
3. *Genuine Opposition*—Accept the critique on your end while presenting your argument. Affirmative statements in self-critique and accepting you were wrong, turns the focus to mediation.
4. *The new dialogue*—Lead the conversation on a positive note toward progress that is mutual.

Let us see a sample debate

Person 1: I really don't think we should continue with the current strategy. It is a failure.
Person 2: What exactly do you find unacceptable? *(Ask for details)*

Person 1: We are going in circles man. This just doesn't make sense. Just scrap it.
Person 2: I agree we have delayed it a lot and it is costing us but I see many long-term benefits. What is the most pressing problem according to you? *(Ask details. Listen to Understand)*

Person 1: I think the design is not good. We are making do with a bad design and, therefore, the rest of the inefficiency is trickling down.

Person 2: While a part of the design needs to be reworked, many parts of the design are great. We have put in many hours toward this and you did love those aspects of the design. Can we rework on the other parts alone? *(Genuine opposition)*

Person 1: It is too much trouble. Too expensive. *(Still debates on this side.)*

Person 2: Maybe we can get help for this part. I know a few vendors. Would you like me speak to them?

Person 1: No. Let us rework on our own. This will mean extra hours.

Person 2: I understand. I am willing to put in that effort. Let me know when we can start. *(The new dialogue)*

Person 1: Let's plan all the changes and do them together in a single effort.

Person 2: Sure sounds like a plan.

Conversation 6

The Perfect Sorry

> *"A stiff apology is a second insult... The injured party does not want to be compensated because he has been wronged; he wants to be healed because he has been hurt"*
>
> **G. K. Chesterton**

There are infinite ways to mess up at work. Missed deadlines, hasty instructions, errors in execution, oversight, and a lack of planning and maybe things are not working smoothly.

Success at work depends on ironing these wrinkles and when something goes wrong, it's important to fix it. When confronting, do not do it from a deficit balance. In other words, do not confront someone if you owe him or her an apology first.

Yes that single word—*sorry* is crucial but there is more to an apology than just a shoulder shrug and a carelessly thrown word.

> **As Mignon McLaughlin says, "True remorse is never just regret over consequences; it is regret over a motive."**

Why is apologizing so difficult?

In a true incident, an acquaintance—let's call her Ramya—had to travel to her client's office in another city on project. Her company handled her travel and stay. When Ramya arrived at her hotel, she was shocked to see the hotel's lack of preparation for her arrival. Her accommodation left a lot to be desired. She complained to the admin department and got a careless answer, "Oh really? I did not know. Send an email and we will get back."

Ramya then escalated her problem to her manager and the issue was resolved within an hour's time.

Why could neither the hotel authorities nor the company's admin department apologize to Ramya?

Why was she left feeling undervalued in a strange city?

Unfortunately, this is not an uncommon situation and many people avoid apologizing because the very idea that they could be wrong, and having to admit it, makes them terribly uncomfortable.

Ryan Fehr, Professor, Foster School of Business observes, "We all like to view ourselves as good people—kind, considerate, and moral." An apology shows us the unacknowledged imperfect version of ourselves that we are not happy acknowledging.

The most difficult parts in an apology are accepting responsibility and letting go.

Accepting Responsibility
By saying *sorry* you are apologizing for your contribution to a situation—that's it.

Apology is the atomic energy of empathy. Failure to apologize is a lapse of integrity that causes the corrosive destruction of your reputation, and leads people to perceive you as arrogant and callous. Accepting the responsibility of action conveys your sincerity and demonstrates courage.

Letting Go
Forgive and forget is easier said than done. Letting go is a step toward healing. It allows you to avoid seeing others' actions through your personal filter of right or wrong. As Henry Boys says—"The most important trip you may take in life is meeting people halfway."

In spite of the virtues of an apology, most *sorrys* leave people filled with anger and a simmering sense of injustice.

The wrong sorry

A sorry without regret is a justification of your actions. Without responsibility, it is an excuse.

When it comes to apologizing, only a sincere apology works although the following apologies are often said begrudgingly;

➤ *A nonapology -*
Lisa Lutz said "I am sorry you're angry, is NOT an apology." Such an apology implies someone's anger has nothing to do with you and that it's an apology without accepting responsibility. "I am sorry I made you angry," will be better welcomed.

➤ *Justification and blame -*
Justification in effect is a denial of the apology and therefore the sorry is fake. "I am sorry for the fight, but in my defense you started it" is blame. Sentences like "Oh! It wasn't that bad" is deflecting consequence and disregarding the other person's feelings.

➤ *Making excuses -*
A sorry that continues with the word *but* is a heavily watered down apology and is therefore ineffective. As

in the feedback, using the word *but* negates the apology. Excuses sometimes do look like a rational explanation. The difference lies in the acknowledgement of responsibility. An explanation without accepting the responsibility is an excuse.

> *Repeating the mistake -*

Even the best-worded apology will be ineffective if the mistake is repeated again. Actions always speak louder than words.

The right sorry

The most constructive structure for an apology is in *The Five Languages of Apology*, a book by Gary Chapman and Jennifer Thomas. They discovered the five fundamental aspects or the *languages* of an apology: expressing regret ("I am sorry"), accepting responsibility ("I was wrong"), making restitution ("What can I do to make it right?"), genuinely repenting ("I'll try not to do that again"), and requesting forgiveness ("Will you please forgive me?").

Another great structure was by Roy Lewicki of The Ohio State University's Fisher College of Business, who led the study to identify the main components of an apology. Their team conducted two studies to explore how seven hundred and fifty five people reacted to apologies, containing one to all six of the components. The list includes: *Expression of regret, explanation of what went wrong, acknowledgement of responsibility, declaration of repentance, offer of repair, and request for forgiveness.*

The most important component was found to be *an acknowledgement of responsibility*, followed by the *offer of repair*. The request for forgiveness was noted to be the least important of all the elements. Therefore, a simple 'I am sorry' is the least effective of all apologies.

Here, with some paraphrasing and modification based on my experiences, are the ingredients of the perfect apology.

1. *Explanation*—Begin with your intention to apologize. This sets the context and the listener becomes receptive to the next words spoken.
2. *Take responsibility*—Be specific about what exactly you are apologizing for, so that there are no vague feelings and the declaration of your responsibility is not lost. For example if you have missed a deadline, be specific about the task and the deadline and not say sorry for your general time management skills.
3. *Express regret*—This is a feelings step. True remorse cannot be hidden, and it is essential to be honestly remorseful. All other apologies are fake.

4. *Promise repair*—As a logical next step to being responsible, offer your solution to rectify the problem. This brings hope to the situation and during most times, creates acceptance in the minds of the listener.
5. *Request for forgiveness*—Finally this step gives the power back to the listener. While it is not necessary to ask for forgiveness, by putting the ball in their court, you have essentially said that the future is up to them.

Exactly what to say

A sample apology for a missed deadline:

I am sorry that I missed the July 7 deadline to submit the reports. I take complete responsibility for the same, as I am the head of the team in charge of this project. Currently, we have completed most of the tasks and I promise to deliver the report by this evening. I sincerely regret the inconvenience caused.

Conversation 7

How to Ask For A Raise and Other Such Conversations

"When we think we lead, we are most led."

Henry James Byron

In an ideal world, your boss will know your worth, will guide you well, work toward your aspirations, and give you a raise. In this world, the unicorns graze alongside the other mythical creatures.

In the real world, however, you have heard it before. You have probably said it repeatedly. People don't quit jobs; they quit their bosses.

Year after year employee surveys indicate that the primary ingredient for job satisfaction is not the job, the salary, or benefits; it is not even the quality of food in the canteen. It is the relationship that the employee has with his boss. So does that mean there are many bad bosses around?

Consider this simple example.

You have been anticipating a raise. You know it is time and that you deserve it. You have worked well. How do you go to your boss to ask for the raise and actually get it?

Was that difficult? How about asking for a promotion, a particular project, or even for a leave of absence? How about asking for feedback? How about telling your boss what you don't like about him or her? How about building a relationship?

Why is this conversation difficult?

We try to make the **boss** difficult when it may be that the **conversation** was a difficult one. Asking for a raise or a promotion is a conversation that has high stakes and, therefore, makes you feel vulnerable. The fear of hearing *no* makes most people avoid these conversations. You may feel like you are pressurizing your boss and are being only self-serving. However, in order to advance your career you need to advocate for yourself.

Not all bosses know how to manage people. Most people are promoted for their technical skills and when it suddenly comes to managing the expectations, aspirations, and limitations of their team many managers are found lacking. So the question to ask now would be how would you manage the manager who manages you?

Your boss matters. As much as you may want to believe that it is your work that will speak for itself, the reality is your boss will heavily influence your success. Therefore having a strong and productive working relationship with your boss is essential for your success.

Third, there is a lot of negativity in the minds of people for managing up talking to your boss to achieve your dreams is considered a cheap way of climbing up the corporate ladder. It is not about political persuasion or 'sucking up'. Managing up is all about taking charge of your career and managing your responsibilities and aspirations in a way that is acceptable to your boss. In the words of Mary Abbajay, "Managing up is about consciously and deliberatively developing and maintaining effective relationships with supervisors, bosses, and other people above you in the chain of command."

It is a deliberate effort to increase cooperation and collaboration in a relationship between individuals who often have different perspectives and uneven power levels.

The most commonly heard negative is—it is the duty of the boss to recognize your efforts, give you that corner office along with a double-digit salary increase. When you learn to manage up successfully, you empower your boss to represent your interests to the influencers in the organization, better.

Managing Up

How do you ask for that raise? Stop believing in those unicorns and learn to manage your career and manage up. Here are some of the strategies to help your way.

> **Focus on why you deserve it and not why you need it.**

Specifically while asking for a raise or a promotion, it is important that you make your boss realize your contribution to the organization. Make sure you are not pitching it as an overdue recognition of your past efforts. The pitch itself should lean more toward the value that you bring in to the organization, and not focus on your past responsibilities and tasks.

Choose the right moment
It is not necessary to wait until the appraisal or promotion time to pitch your interests. That is the period when your boss is also carrying time and budget constraints. A heads up, specifically before you take on new responsibilities is a good start.

Regular feedbacks
Ask your boss for regular feedback and advice on how you can get to the next level. As a continual process, ask for feedback. When you feel like you are ready for a promotion or a raise, your boss already knows your interests and he will be responsible for your efforts.

Be prepared to hear No
In spite of all the preparation, you may still hear a no. Don't be discouraged by a no.

If you don't get your pay raise, the next promotion, or that particular project you wanted, it doesn't have to be the end of the negotiation process. Work around the possibilities. Ask for better benefits if it is a rejection for an increment on your salary, ask for a better project if it is a promotion and if you get a no for a project, ask for feedback and work on your skills.

While the way to the heart of the raise is clear, look for these pitfalls to avoid while managing up:

- Do not assume that asking for a promotion is a one-time discussion. It is the same with any

form of asking. Build your case in a series of conversations to make your boss understand your value and to build the correct rapport.
- Do not play the "other offer" card. Do not throw ultimatums or threaten to leave the company even in humor. That tactic often has a negative impact on professional relationships.
- Do not get discouraged if you don't get what you want right away. Be patient.

Other similar conversations

In the current VUCA world, organizations face the pressure of revenue targets constantly. With the fluctuating growth, recruitment freezes, and rising automation it has become equally difficult to ask your boss for an extra resource.

The typical manager works on a thinly stretched budget and it may look like your team of three is doing the work of eight. When you are able to offer a shoulder to the heavily burdened wheel and deliver, it is but a difficult task to make your manager realize the need for a new resource.

So how do you tell your manager that you are understaffed? For it is not a sustainable solution. The team will look for options outside and thus the organization loses good talent. The current team can burnout and thus decrease productivity.

On the other end of this spectrum is a new and innovative project that you want to start. The already stretched budget makes every new suggestion an uphill battle with your manager. How do you convince and persuade your line manager that this idea is important?

Do you get replies like, "We already have too much on our plate. The team cannot deliver this extra load"

Or a more polite version like, "Your idea is good but our current strategy is to cut costs. This project may not work in line with the current organization strategy."

Such lines though true, ensure that your idea dies a slow and quiet death.

Exactly what to say

<u>To your boss while asking for a raise:</u>
I would like to discuss with you a few of my responsibilities with the organization and my aspirations, can you spare a few minutes? (Set the context and ask for permission)

I have worked on these projects recently and as we have discussed earlier, my contribution has been fruitful (be specific here) to the organization.

I feel that I bring in value to the organization and with the current additions to my responsibility, I request you to review my current salary. (Pause and listen to the response.)

State your value (Come prepared. None of your arguments should be negative.)

Finally, negotiate the amount and other benefits along with the salary.

<u>How to ask for another team member?</u>
Raghav, I would like to speak with you on the current team performance. Can we meet for a few minutes?

(yes)

Raghav, I am sure you will agree that currently our team of three is doing a lot of work. Because of the understaffed situation, we are facing issues. (Write down what's currently not getting completed as a result of not having that extra staffing slot.)

We will require another technical team member with (be specific) qualifications to manage the current and future projects. (Write down what additional things your team would achieve if they had that spot filled.)

I am bringing this to your notice now as I can clearly see the team stretching themselves every day in order to meet the deadlines. An additional member will motivate the team. We also have three new projects for the coming months and having a resource now will be the right time to train and bring them on par with the team.

(Your boss can argue back with budget issues or the time of hire. Please feel free to tweak the conversation to suit your need.)

Conversation 8

The Loquacious One

"Brevity is the best recommendation of speech whether in a senator or an orator."

Marcus Tullius Cicero

It is worth repeating at this point the theories that Ford had come up with, on his first encounter with human beings, to account for their peculiar habit of continually stating and restating the very obvious, as in "It's a nice day," or "You're very tall," or "So this is it, we're going to die."

His first theory was that if human beings didn't keep exercising their lips, their mouths probably shriveled up.

After a few months of observation he had come up with a second theory, which was this—"If human beings don't keep exercising their lips, their brains start working." This interesting point from the book, *The Restaurant at the End of the Universe* by Douglas Adams gives the humorous yet apt view of our speaking abilities.

We all know someone who talks a lot. We may be that someone who talks too much. Loquacious people are common in society. In fact *speaking* is one of the most important survival abilities of humans. A person who talks a lot is the heart of the party. The problem occurs when there is a little too much talk, and there is no space for others in that conversation.

What can we do about them? And maybe more important is what can you do if you happen to *be* one of them?

Why keep it short?

The best kinds of conversations are when people say "we spoke for hours together and never knew how time flew" but the reality is brevity has its strength.

The most important reason to keep any speech short is the reducing attention span. Do you know we are currently fighting our attention span with a goldfish? That on an average we can focus only for about eight seconds before another thought hits us? With this statistic, anyone speaking for a long time has lost his or her audience's attention too long ago.

The more important your message is the shorter should your speech be in order to keep the attention of your audience focused on the topic.

> **Communication expert Alan Weiss says, "People have the tendency to tell others everything they know," instead of what is required. Along talk is filled with excessive information and, therefore, results in a dilution of content when someone speaks too long on a topic.**

Imagine if you were a doctor who had to ask your patient "what happened" and have to listen to the following:

"I had to go to a wedding of a relative. We actually went to my childhood home city and since I am visiting the city after ten long years, I was uncontrollable. The wedding food was amazing and I think I ate a bit too much. My relatives were so loving and nice, they insisted on serving extra every time the plate was empty. Actually, my relatives are all very close. We have so many WhatsApp groups it is difficult to remember. We also went shopping the day before and I had a great meal. I loved everything about it but now my stomach hurts."

If every doctor had to hear the whole week's story for every stomachache and earache, he or she might give up his or her degree. The simple problem statement gets lost in all the trivial news and your problem, therefore, becomes trivial.

A long winding conversation tends to move toward topics other than the current one. We have heard talks that begin with the weekend, and end up with how difficult their last project was and why they are looking out for a job. Insecurity and anxiety makes people speak more but it is also a compulsive trait of many.

The most important requirement to keep the conversation short is because a long talk is a drain on your positive energy. If the topic requires an hour's lecture and it is prepared, that is different. An unplanned small talk moving on to a never-ending gab is a drain on energy for both the speaker and the listener.

Sometimes the liberal talker adds on personal euphemisms like "honey," "sweetie," "dear" while talking to strangers and at many times the receiver is comfortable with the familiarity in the vocabulary. However, there can be instances where the over familiarity can be considered offensive. It is specific to mention here that when a male colleague speaks to his female colleague with such words it can be considered sexual harassment. In such cases, you are the ripe low hanging fruit in a litigation battle. For when the complaints are written, the first things that get noticed are the choice of words.

Finally, a lot of talking results in the universal human problem of gossip. Snippets of conversations often hit you during your break time, meetings, or in the corridor. Under the cloak of a friendly chat, the dagger pierces someone's character, plans, vulnerability, or privacy. Even if the gossip is untrue, it could damage multiple reputations or at least hurt feelings. Yet such workplace behaviors go unchecked and unaddressed under the guise of *grapevining*.

How to keep it short?

If you are a loquacious talker, be aware that you tend to speak stories at the slightest encouragement. Awareness is the first step. According to Dan Brule, "Awareness allows us to get outside of our mind and observe it in action." The following three steps can be used to avoid the long wind.

Plan ahead

Prepare ahead of time, what you may want to speak before actually speaking. While every conversation need not be like a well-edited speech or sound robotic, a basic preparation while keeping the discussion short will allow for spontaneity as well.

Be sensitive to audience signals

Listen to your audience while you speak. Do you find them losing interest? Look at their body language. Are they losing focus while looking at you? Are they distracted? Do their eyes, gestures, and body language give the impression that they want to move ahead? Please check your speaking to notice these things. In case your audience is interested, they will nod, smile, and ask pertinent questions. In the absence of these signals, you know that disinterest has crept in and, therefore, you must end your talk.

Remember your why

At all times during a conversation be aware of why you are speaking, what you are speaking. This is the easiest way to avoid going into the zone of speaking about unwanted things. Your *why* keeps you out of the weeds.

Exactly what to say

To a person who talks too much
Sorry I am interrupting. Can you please tell me specifically your ailment? (As a doctor to the patient above)

Sorry I know I am interrupting but I have had a long day and I am ready to crash, do you think we can continue tomorrow. I would really love to hear your experience but right now, I am tired.

To a person who uses many personal euphemisms

Sid, I'd like to talk to you about a situation that came by today. Are you free for a couple of minutes?

(Yes)

Thanks. I know you have a great working relationship with your team and that the team loves your inputs. However, a few members are not very comfortable with you referring to them with personal euphemisms like kiddo, sweetie, or dear. I am not asking you to change your personality but it is a good business practice to keep the familiar vocabulary to the friends' circle alone.

To a group when unwanted gossip about any person is spread

Hi team, I have Raghav with me in this meeting. There have been a few conversations and rumors about his personal life. I have no idea how the information originated and if anyone would like to speak with me in private after this meeting, you are welcome.

However, I would like to say such conversations are hurtful and we as a team need to raise our voices against rumors spread about personal lives that have no bearing to the performance of the member.

It is not important if the rumor is true or false; it's about the respect of a fellow team member.

Conversation 9

Stay in The Game, Listen

"By understanding the way conversations impact our listening we can determine how we listen—and how we listen determines how we interpret and make sense of our world."

Judith E. Glaser

It was Dr. Joyce Brothers who said, "Listening, not imitation, may be the sincerest form of flattery." Listening is the best way to respond to any conversation. It encourages the speaker and enables you to understand what they are saying.

Listening is the most underdeveloped skill in communication. Many believe that they are good listeners, but it is largely mistaken for hearing.

We have established that not every conversation is communication; similarly, hearing does not equate to listening. Hearing is a very superficial activity of cognitively understanding the spoken words.

Listening hard is what the practitioners call active listening and it is hard to practice.

Why is Active Listening difficult?

The very definition of listening is understood to be hearing, with a bit of thinking. To quote Mark Goulsten, author of the book *Just Listen*, "True listening, isn't something that merely happens to you. It is something to do and to feel, to throw yourself into rationally, emotionally, and physically. Listening is something that engages us with multiple senses. It isn't passive or reactive; it's creative. And to do it well, you must feel the experience—not just think about it."

Active listening is to understand why a person is saying something. It involves not just the what aspect but also replying to the why aspect.

It is difficult because we are interrupted in many ways. Our emotions, aspirations, and judgments often come in the way of listening.

Consider this conversation:

Ahaana: I am so excited today. We have booked tickets to go to the Disneyland in Florida. We plan to be there for a whole week.

Mita: That's great. Disneyland is a great choice. I vacationed there a couple years back.

Superficially, this conversation does not sound bad, but if there were *true listening* from Mita's end, she would have listened to the excitement and the need to share the news. True listening would have changed the reply to,

Mita: Oh I am so glad for you. Seven days in Disneyland? That's so exciting. What are your plans?

Let us consider another conversation:

Sid: I want to quit

Raghav: Hey! Things are not so bad. You will come out as a winner. Trust me. Don't talk about quitting.

Superficially, this reply appears to be motivating, but to a man who is ready to throw in the towel, it will sound like the listener is downplaying his emotional state.

The first response in each example is to reply by telling the speaker how they should feel or what they should do; express approval or disapproval.

Replies like these seldom help or satisfy those who confide in you. Instead, it generally makes your speaker feel that you don't really want to get involved or that you don't trust them or their problems.

If you actively listen to Sid in the above conversation, you will hear his dejection, his fear in quitting, and his loss of faith in being able to pull through. In such a situation, we are not in his shoes, therefore, any form of suggestions regarding what to do is wrong.

Let's do this conversation once again with active listening -

Sid: I want to quit.
Raghav: The job means a lot to you, doesn't it?
Sid: Yeah, my appraisal this time sucked and I am scared I will lose my job.
Raghav: You are worried how it will affect your life.

Such active listening builds trust and allows the person to open up. Having their problems understood, reflected, not judged, and decreed shows that you have faith in their ability to arrive at their own solutions.

You are not a walking, talking motivational wallpaper on a search engine. Let's stop sounding like one.

> **Most people don't come to us for a solution, but for a shoulder.**

Where to use Active Listening?

A simple point would be everywhere although some places require it more.

Active listening is the best way to keep the conversation going. You will see people becoming overjoyed at the chance to express themselves without being cut off by some glib comment. This is the foundation of a great relationship.

Active listening is especially important when your speaker has something emotional to say. Happiness, grief, worry, and anger are all equally important emotions that deserve an active ear.

Try to be interested instead of interesting—your speaker will expect you to be interested in what he has to say. That is the reason he opened up to you. By trying to be interesting you are fulfilling a self-serving act and this will not really strengthen the relationship. Slowly they will stop sharing emotional issues with you.

Practicing active listening, however, needs to be approached with caution. Once people realize you are an active listener, honest criticisms may creep out of the closet. People may want to say, "Now that you are really listening, I want to say..." It would be easier to be prepared for such surprises. The most important act at this point is to be silent and let their emotion run.

As Winston Churchill says, "Criticism may not be agreeable, but it is necessary. It fulfills the same function as pain in the human body. It calls attention to an unhealthy state of things." Listening to what others have to say, will be useful to your development.

In business, active listening is the soul of negotiation. Listening to what is being said in totality—the emotion, the facts, the body language, and the unsaid words will give us an edge in understanding the team across the table.

Active listening will make them open up more and, therefore, you have more cards on the table to make a better and informed decision.

Further, the trust built in the process will ensure smoother business processes where both parties are satisfied.

Ultimately, active listening helps to build a rapport and trust, which then can allow a negotiation move toward the next step of jointly exploring options that can lead to an agreement.

Exactly what to say

Sid: I hate your behavior. You are not the 'be all' in my life.
Raghav: I am sorry my words upset you. I should have listened to you.

Sid: You heard me right. It's just that you ignore my views.
Raghav: What I feel about your views is important to you. Please know that your views are important to me too.

Sid: But you did not listen to them.
Raghav: I did. We can run through them again but please remember I will question everything. Is that ok?

Sid: Yeah, I have issues with being questioned. I flare up when anyone questions me.
Raghav: I do not doubt you. I am just working on the idea.

Sid: I understand. Let's do this again.

Conversation 10

You Are What You Ask

"The unexamined life is not worth living."

Socrates

What did Socrates, Buddha, Jesus, and Shakespeare have in common? According to Sobel and Panas, they all knew how to ask powerful questions.

In my class or in coaching, I can always tell who the interested, experienced audience is by listening to the questions they ask. Living in a world of answers, we often forget our mind stretches to find answers only to the questions it is asked.

Therefore, good questions are far more important than answers.

Questions challenge our thinking and motivate us to look for newer answers. In ancient times, philosophers like Socrates used questions extensively to bring change. Their questions were teaching tools, and a means to change indelibly the people around them. Even today, a stream called Socratic teaching is a teaching method executed through questioning.

It is no accident that the most famous dramatic passage in all of literature is built around a single question; "to be, or not to be, that is the question," says Shakespeare's Prince Hamlet, as he contemplates life and death.

Why is *the question* a very scary villain in our conversations? Why do people not like them? In fact, most will avoid asking and answering even the most mundane questions.

Why is asking a difficult part of a conversation?

The true intention of a question is to make people curious enough to know the answer. To move away from feeling the problem to analyzing the problem.

Dr. Marilee Adams, author of the book *Change your Questions, Change your Lives,* calls this the learner and the judger mindset. Asking questions from the judger mindset will neither solve the problem nor will it facilitate any collaboration.

> **For true questions to emerge, and for the mind to become curious enough to find solutions, questions should be from the learner mindset—curious enough to know the unknown.**

The difficulty arises when we don't ask questions from the place of curiosity but from many other unfavorable locations.

Questions asked to judge or test a person are often very toxic to the relationship.
Consider the conversation -
"Why have you not broken down the costs in slide three?"

This is not a question. It is an accusation. The judgment that something is being either hidden, or not worked properly, is clear in the question. The implicit question here is

"Have you really done the calculation or is it a guess? Or are you hiding something?"

Such questions will immediately garner defensive answers. But these questions pose as rationally curious ones in the corporate world. However much you would like to respond with rudeness, a better strategy would be to rephrase the question in your mind, and respond to the more positive formulation. Respond to the question, not the accusation.

Questions asked to express disagreement or to even exert power.

Consider the question,

"Can you give me one good reason why I should agree to this?"

It is a question filled with power and distinctly shows disagreement. In fact, these types of questions should come with a danger signal of some kind, as even after answering them well; the people involved will not leave the table with satisfaction, but with ego and pride alone. These are actually controlling statements masquerading as questions. The response the questioner wants may not be an answer but an argument. A good argument sometimes is great and refreshing although not reacting to the statement but softly responding will get better results.

Yet sometimes in conversations, we feel like we are being interviewed for a job. A series of questions hits us and makes the whole experience awkward. Consider this conversation-

- "Hi, when did to move to this city?"
- "Hi, it's been a couple years now."
- "So how do you find the change?"
- "Not bad. We expected the differences"
- "So where are the kids studying?"
- "At ABC school"
- "Where are you working?"
- "In an IT firm"

- "So where do you live now?"

This is not a conversation. It is more like someone is noting facts about me for some purpose and that is scary. We see such interrogations at social events and it is often frustrating. No one likes being questioned so much. Instead, the conversation could have taken off after the first question into how the city is improving or on any other common ground.

The problem the questions above, are that they were not asked with the intent to know the answer. Therefore, they are not really powerful questions.

The most important statement masquerading as question and as a woman I have to agree is, "If a woman asks 'Do I look fat in this dress?' they are not asking for an answer, they are asking for a *compliment*." Very insightful, don't you agree?

The Powerful Questions

In business and in life, the powerful questions are the ones that actually get results. Questions like "How is it going?" may sound positive but are too vague for the listener to tell you any of the problems.

Such vague questions are typically answered with vague sentences like "All set boss. We are great."

When the deadlines are not met, other vague questions will follow,

"Why is the deadline slipping?"

Vague answer—"We are working on it, we will be done by today"

In all these questions, the person who asked the question has had no concrete answer. This is not empowerment. Powerful questions get into the heart of the matter, and ensure that the answers given are also concrete.

Exactly what to say (ASK)

While asking for details, use specific descriptive questions that elicit a detailed and specific answer –

Instead of asking –
How is the project shaping up Sid?

Try asking –
Sid, can you please take me through the work done on the ABC project so far? Further, can we please run through your schedule for the implementation?

While clarifying or taking decisions –
Instead of asking -
Explain your case (makes the question an accusation)

Try asking –
That's an interesting thought, what process did you go through to reach that conclusion?

Conversation 11

Emotional Outbursts, Temper, and Foul Language

"Emotions are built on layers. Beneath hatred is usually anger; beneath anger is frustration; beneath frustration is hurt; beneath hurt is fear. If you keep expressing your feelings, you will generally move through them in that order. What begins with "I hate you" culminates in "I'm scared. I don't want to lose you, and I don't know what to do about it."

Mark Goulston,
Get Out of Your Own Way:
Overcoming Self-Defeating Behavior

The day began on a downward spiral. In fact, it has been a series of bad days this entire month. You are reviewing a project report of your team. It is substandard, and one that you just cannot submit to your boss. The same boss who has been expecting miracles out of you while assigning a bunch of low paid below average team members.

Your feedback on the project report is not received well. You start to shout out. Your team is going to remember you calling them 'half assed morons.' You have to meet HR, your boss, and yes continue to work amicably with your team.

What do you do?

In the above scenario, you can be the angry team leader, the harassed team, the manager, or the pacifying HR. When workplace outbursts occur, it is always messy.

Did I hear you murmur that such things don't happen in real life? They do and frequently so in many teams.

During her ten years as chief executive of eBay, Meg Whitman, was known for sharp bursts of anger toward employees whose work or preparation she found to be lacking. In June 2007, an eBay employee Ms. Kim, claimed that Ms. Whitman became angry and forcefully pushed her into an executive conference room at eBay's headquarters. This was also according to multiple former eBay employees with knowledge of the incident. Ms. Kim, who was not injured in the incident hired a lawyer and threatened to file a lawsuit, but the dispute was resolved under the supervision of a private mediator. (*Source: NY Times*)

Yes, in your argument it is true that the workplace today has become a fertile petri-dish breeding stress and emotionally intense lives. As a result, a few outbursts have become common. The flatter structure, more informal work culture, and the constant pressure to succeed have made the use of foul language, common.

> **The etiquette that is inherently part of every culture around the world stands diluted in the global workplace today.**

The HR does have rules stating it is professionally uncouth to spew foul words and, therefore, at such times the emotion that comes out is passive aggression. The glaring eyes, a throbbing vein on the forehead, the clenched jaw line, or the static silence are all signs of passive aggression. It really does not matter how the emotional bursts happen, but when they do, there is a lot left to be handled professionally.

The crier, the screamer, the table pounder or the silent glarer, are all detrimental actions that affect the team performance. An emotional reaction is a clue that the issue you are discussing is touching a sensitive topic. Therefore, the difficulty lies in the emotions versus the facts.

Why is an emotional outburst difficult?

How will you speak with the team that you just called morons? Professionalism aside, this kind of behavior is detrimental to any interpersonal relationship. What do you do now that you are the villain of every conversation around the smoking corner or the water cooler?

You apologize. You say sorry as it has been explained in this book and then go back to work because "You could have been the most charming colleague for twenty years, but have an outburst on just one day and that's all people will remember," says Mark Jeffries, international management consultant and author of *The Art of Business Seduction*.

> **"You can't put lava back in the volcano."**

It is difficult for the manager or even the mediating HR to handle an emotional outburst. Imagine the team complaining to you and the HR, about the angry outburst above. You know the team is upset and you search for the pacifying answers.

Unfortunately, your response brings out more anger in the team. Why?

Because in your eagerness to calm your angry members you put on a smile, speak with a calm moral superiority that comes across as extremely patronizing.

A few quick don'ts in such a situation as the mediator will be-

Never quote company policy. This is yet to move toward a legal battle; don't push it to one. Emotions can be dealt, without the legalese.

Further, try not to point out the smaller and minor errors in their complaints. Sentences like "actually you are exaggerating. It was a ten minute meeting at 5:00 p.m. and not a half hour meeting at 5:30 p.m." will trigger intense emotions against you.

Lastly, it is advisable not to ask them to remain calm. That sounds like telling a child he has a time out. It is really not necessary to have a fake soft and sweet voice. Research says that fake happy faces puts off people more than a genuine angry outburst.

Exactly what to say

When someone starts shouting or even talking intense, it is an instinct to assume the person is mad (emotionally angry) and many are uncomfortable with strong emotions.

Be genuinely concerned
The initial step is to become aware of the emotion. Not take the emotion away by brushing it off with a smile but rather to embrace it as a human aspect. Acting calm with a fake smile will be perceived as if you don't care.

Humans get angry. It is as important an emotion, as happiness is. Once you are aware of the emotion, listen deeply to the hurt, the confusion, and the stress. The most important step now is to ask questions to clarify your understanding and maybe even create a rapport.

Underline the bottom line
After allowing the person to voice their emotion, slowly build to the bottom line. At the end of the day, having a working relationship is important. The angry employee and his latest victim both need to understand that they need to work in the same location, together every day.

Be careful to underscore their mutual purpose in the organization.

Resolve the problem
Finally get into the facts, discuss options to solve the issues, to ensure both parties come to an understanding.

One last thing to think about is to make sure people understand,

> **Emotions are in the immediate present, but their actions will reflect well into their far distant future as well.**

[This conversation does not have a conversation script in this section and the *Exactly what to say* is explained in a general way as each person's emotion is different and I trust with the process above, you can speak specifically to your issue in life.]

Conversation 12

Delivering Bad News

"Nothing travels faster than the speed of light with the possible exception of bad news, which obeys its own special laws."

Douglas Adams

At some point in our lives, we all have to deliver bad news. It can be break ups in college, loss of a loved one as we grow older, or even a job loss. Some professions need to give more than their share of bad news.

The HR managers may feel like part of their soul gets ripped every time they have to lay off employees, but an oncologist has an even worse job of informing loved ones that his patient is diagnosed with cancer.

As quoted by Sophocles, *"No one loves the messenger who brings bad news."* Shooting the messenger is the apt metaphor in many places to show the resistance that people have to deliver bad news.

An early literary citing of "shooting the messenger" is in Plutarch's *Lives states*: "The first messenger, that gave notice of Lucullus' coming was so far from pleasing Tigranes that, he had his head cut off for his pains; and no man dared to bring further information. Without any intelligence at all, Tigranes sat while war was already blazing around him, giving ear only to those who flattered him." (*Source: Wikipedia*)

Why is delivering bad news difficult?

The very nature of the news is a difficult one. That one reason should be enough to make the process difficult. Yet, the conversation gets compounded in its difficulty by delivering the news in an inappropriate manner.

It is worse in healthcare. Breaking bad news is one of the doctor's most difficult duties, yet medical education typically offers little formal training for this daunting task.

In 1847, the American Medical Association's first code of medical ethics stated, "The life of a sick person can be shortened not only by the acts but also by the words or the manner of a physician. It is therefore a sacred duty to guard himself carefully in this respect and to avoid all things that have a tendency to discourage the patient and to depress his spirits." In the last hundred and seventy-one years sadly, doctors still are unsure regarding how to talk to patients. Doctor's may not like to give the bad news and take away hope. However, it is an important part of communication.

In most other industries as well, they begin with a vague small talk and then find a path half way to deliver bad news. This is one of the many errors that we make.

> **Combine vague talk and beating around the bush with information and the listener is going to hear the bad news in a slow torturous manner.**

No one wants to hear disappointing stuff for an hour. Brevity is your soul here.

During the financial meltdown in the year 2008, many employees were laid off. Whole sales teams were made redundant. In one such unfortunate circumstance, an acquaintance's company had to lay off almost a third of its employees.

The senior management decided to call the few senior managers who will be staying on and asked them to be the ones to lay off their team members. Needless to say no manager was prepared on what to say at such times.

One manager, a young person, was facing such a situation for the first time. He froze. His conversation went something on the lines of:

> Manager: Vikas.
> Vikas: (waiting)
> Manager: I guess it is goodbye.
> Vikas: (In shock though it was expected given the economy.)
> Manager: Don't worry, you will find another job soon.
> Vikas: (mumbles something)
> Manager: In fact, let us catch up in the evening and look into your resume, ok?
> Vikas: (silently gets up to go)

Apart from the fact that this was a very wrong way to deliver any news of such brevity, the vagueness of the news will keep Vikas guessing the complete meaning of the message for a long time.

Sentences like *'Don't worry, you will find another job soon'* trivializes the situation. For the employee, it is a grave one. Being fired is like a permanent hit to your self-esteem.

The most glaring error in the supposed conversation above is the unwanted and unasked advice. One that is vague again. An offer for help to look into the resume? It rings of a person trying to say something quick to just escape the current situation.

Such meetings are inherently awkward. The feelings of shame, inadequacy, and disappointment linger in the air like a thick black cloud.

Let us now discuss time. Bad news cannot be wished away, by keeping quiet. It is a ticking bomb and will blow over sometime. Delayed bad news is bigger bad news. Therefore, to immediately inform is the best thing to do. It will not come as a surprise if the news is given on time. If the employees are surprised by bad news, managers are not fulfilling their responsibilities.

Bad news is not permission for people to be rude or disrespectful. We are not just communicating bad news; we are communicating it to human beings.

Exactly what to say

In case of firing employees:

Vikas, I am sorry we have to let you go. This is an organization-wide restructuring process and does not reflect personally on your individual capability in the organization.

You have been a great member of the team and we would like you to leave on friendly terms.

I have a set of logistics for your release (Keep them ready.)

You have the next three weeks to complete your release and handover duties. I hope we can assist you in finding a better job and remember you will be getting a good reference from us.

Conversation 13

The Undiscussables—Responding To Personal Probes

"A man is likely to mind his own business when it is worth minding. When it is not, he takes his mind off his own meaningless affairs by minding other people's business."

Eric Hoffer

There is one in every family, every neighborhood, and every office—the common species called the nosy ones.

Curiosity killed the cat. And now the curious people kill our peace of mind. In many cases, the curious people are just an annoyance, but sometimes the nosy questions are hurtful or downright judgmental.

Imagine going to a parlor to get your hair styled (both men and women.) You look forward to the soothing music from those built-in speakers and dream that your hairline is finally going to make you look ten years younger. But the minute the stylist touches your hair, begins the barrage of questions.

- What kind of shampoo do you use?
- How many times a week do you wash your hair?
- Do you have a demanding job?

The worst feeling is you cannot even walk out but need to pretend to be sleepy or reply with some vague answer.

We live in the open information world of Facebook, Twitter, and Instagram where all our activities are aired in Technicolor. That is no permission to be intrusive.

> **There's a difference between what we choose to share and what we want to be asked to share.**

Whether it is a well-meaning aunt prying about your love life, parents, or in-laws persistently asking when they'll be grandparents, friends asking about the cost of your house, colleagues inquiring about your salary and bonus or friends asking about your weight gain, the questions can be intrusive and many times inappropriate.

A friend who runs a startup on infertility and its social fallouts says the shame of not being able to procreate is the most difficult feeling for many women, rather than the actual situation of not being able to have kids.

People ask ridiculously personal questions like "So are you trying hard?" (Did they really mean to ask the number of times someone had to *try*?)

How do you respond to such blatantly intrusive questions?

In their defense, there are a few overtly extroverted people in the human species that thrive on the well of continuous flowing personal information to survive. From their side, they wouldn't mind being asked the nosy questions too. They honestly would not have meant to intrude but their sense of personal space may not be the same as yours. Polite answers would generally be enough in such cases.

The difficulty arises when the nosiness turns to nastiness. There may be three types of nastiness cloaked in nosiness.

The chatty user
These are the overly friendly colleagues, who talk about everything and are the heart of the corridor gossips. The trouble comes in when the behavior changes from curiosity, to thinking information is power, and trying to use it against you. It can range from jokes about what you said or did, to blackmail in extreme cases. To such people the information about their environment is their security.

The lingering stalker
They can be in the physical world or virtual. That office colleague who sneaks up behind you silently waiting for you to finish, is a distraction in your work. If they are overly polite, you can request them firmly to walk up to you and ask if you are free to talk. You could say, "I understand you want to wait for me to finish but I am always busy. Going forward, if you want to speak with me please walk right in and ask. If I am busy I will let you know."

The problematic ones are the people who want to know what you do, right from every email you send. This can be a fan in the making but it can equally be a stalker.

Online such people keep following everything you do. Careful security and posting, to ensure that only the stuff that is for the public eye is accessible, can help as a starting point.

The veiled envy
Not every nosy person is curious. Some are jealous. Some are old friends, estranged spouses, ex colleagues, jealous neighbors, and friends who have simply have not let go of you.

Such people can both stalk you, and ask personal questions. These questions will be heavily veiled in sarcasm to make you feel low about yourself.

How do you respond to such blatant intrusions in your life? Do you stammer out a vague response? Shout at them to mind their own business? (sometimes people deserve it, but it may not be the right solution.)

Exactly what to say

We've all been there, and it's tricky to decide in the heat of the moment how best to react or respond.

Here are a few key strategies for handling difficult conversational moments with grace, while keeping the particulars of your personal life private.

Be silent
These are the times when silence is the greatest part of communication. The long pause will say more than any words. Your silence says this particular topic is not up for discussion. Most people will get it. In case some don't, please look at the other options.

Try humor
Humor is a light way to dissuade, and can make even your sharp answer bearable and polite.

So the next time someone asks you, "What is your salary?" try answering this:

"A lot less than I am worth."

In case people want to know when you will get married, try humor "I am waiting for my dream girl."

Try honesty
It is the most direct approach. The tricky part is your emotions. Honestly, you are irritated and, therefore, your tone of voice may convey your hard feelings. Honest answers are the simplest answers. One of the most common intrusions occurs when a colleague takes leave for a day.

"Why did you not come to office yesterday?" is on the lips of the entire gossip brigade.

Try honesty, "I took a day off for personal reasons."

Yes, it is quite possible that some will probe further asking you to elaborate on personal reason. "That is why the reason stated is personal. I would prefer to not discuss the details."

Conversation 14

Ruminations—The Hurtful Mental Reruns

"Are you willing to take responsibility for your mistakes—and for the attitudes and actions that led to them?' Then he said, 'Are you willing—however begrudgingly—to forgive yourself, and even laugh at yourself?' And finally, 'Will you look for value in your experiences, especially the most difficult ones?' Bottom line, 'Are you willing to learn from what happened and make changes accordingly?"

Marilee G. Adams,
Change Your Questions, Change Your Life
10 Powerful Tools for Life and Work

Do you remember that story of what happened to you last month? How you were wronged last year? How badly your in-laws, boss, or your spouse treated you five years ago?

Are you angry now?

If you are still holding on to the hurtful threads from your memory of the past, you are in deep resentment.

Resentment is that gnawing feeling that you were treated unfairly at some point in the past. It can be an overlooked promotion, disrespectful relatives, neglecting family or even society.

Maybe you are still expecting some of these people from your past to come and apologize to you, maybe even change their behavior and appreciate or acknowledge that you were wronged in some manner.

While anger is a strong emotion and exhaustion often limits its tenure, resentment is like the embers of the fire and can burn your gut and life for many years.

The repeated mental replays of the old arguments and unfair treatment keep you in a vicious loop of negativity. This negativity then becomes a behavior and begins to reflect in all your conversations.

Consider this situation that has become a common joke with millions of memes. "All that you speak with your wife will be recorded internally only to be used back against you at opportune moments." This fictitious example is for us to see the other side as well.

You are coming back home after a very long, exhaustive day at work and want to just crash in front of the TV, catch the match highlights, and doze off.

The minute you enter the house your spouse shouts, "Do you know what your son did today at school?"

She continues, "He has not completed any class work this entire week."

You are in no mood to supervise homework and ask "Why?"

"Because he thinks he is too smart, that's why."

Any argument or pacifying statement at this moment will blow up this situation.

The arguments mercurially escalate to, "What do you know about parenting? Apart from paying the fees you don't do anything. Do you have any idea what my day looks like? No. You are married to your job. I am behaving like a single parent household here. When was the last time you asked me how my day went? Or easy question, which extra class does your son go to on Wednesday?"

Now you wish you were still at work.

This is the result of the repeated build-up of resentment. Each incident linked to the previous one, is a chain full of past anger, burning slowly.

Research says that we think close to seventy-thousand thoughts every day. The sad part is over 95 percent of them are thoughts that were repeated from yesterday. The mental reruns of negative thoughts can take up to 95 percent of your psychological time.

The problem with playing these mind movies from the past is that our brain tends to associate the past emotion even in the present situations. This is what happened to the yelling spouse in the above example.

She is probably stretched, fears if her son will grow up to be a responsible adult, feels neglected and unloved; and these emotions burst at a simple "*why?*"

It might seem like she was waiting for the slightest crack in the conversation to launch all that was bottled up inside of her.

Newton said in his laws of motion—"For every action there is an equal and opposite reaction."

What are your mental reruns—the unfair boss, the lost promotion, the missed opportunity, your never ending workload, or your team's behavior?

For these parallel resentments in your mind, your spouse's verbal barrages pour fuel to your embers. Fire now blasts from your side:

"Go ahead, earn what I do. Maybe then you will appreciate me more."

Or if your spouse is also working, *"Listen I don't get an easy workload like you do, where I can pay attention to every letter that my son writes. I have an important meeting tomorrow, so please stop your venom."*

And then in both of your memories another resentment links itself to the already long chain.

Steven Stosny, author of the book *Empowered Love: Use Your Brain to Be Your Best Self and Create Your Ideal Relationship* says, "Dragging the chain of resentment through life is like carrying around a bag of horse manure. You want to smear the bag of horse do-do in the face of the person you resent. So you carry it around waiting for the opportunity and carry it around, and carry it around, and carry it around.

And ultimately who stinks?"

Exactly what to say

> **Marshall Goldsmith puts it simply—"Don't live in the now; invest in your future." This means we put a tight lid on the chain of resentment and talk only about the future for we are yet to mess with it.**

It is a very difficult act to forgive and forget. Many might even want to think of this as losing to your enemy, but let us acknowledge that enemy lies within us. Whether you forgive and forget or actually confront the person responsible or apologize for your role in the situation, a few conversation rules will help you in your way. In the words of Shannon L. Alder, "The more you talk about it, rehash it, rethink it, cross analyze it, debate it, respond to it, get paranoid about it, compete with it, complain about it, immortalize it, cry over it, kick it, defame it, stalk it, gossip about it, pray over it, put it down, or dissect its motives the more it continues to rot in your brain. It is dead. It is over. It is gone. It is done. It is time to bury it because it is smelling up your life, and no one wants to be near your rotted corpse of memories and decaying attitude. Be the funeral director of your life and bury that thing!"

Future Speak -

In the example above, you may want to say, "From

now on, I would appreciate if we can have this conversation an hour after I come home. I am mentally exhausted by the time I come home and I will be a better support to you once I unwind."

Conversation 15

The Chilling Silence

"All that is needed for evil to triumph is for good people to say nothing."

**Eli Wiesel,
Nobel Laureate**

We are raised by a frightened society that believes in the virtues of silence: "Better to be quiet and be thought a fool than to talk and be known as one." Or the one I have heard a million times since childhood—"Speech is silver but silence is golden."

Silence is a virtue and it is often associated with modesty, respect for others, maturity, decorum, even acceptance. These social virtues are now reinforced in the organization by keeping quiet about ideas, opinions, and decisions.

Silence begins when we choose not to confront. There may be a bit of positivity in choosing your battles; but silence becomes a detriment to the team when used during a brainstorming session. The very idea of a brainstorming session is to come out with a variety of ideas, each one different from the other. In such times, remaining silent kills the team's performance. The pressure for unanimity can prevent employees of roughly equal grade and status—even top managers—from exploring their differences.

Micheal Beer, chairman and founder of TruePoint—a research based management consultancy and Canners-Rabb, professor of Business Administration, Emeritus at the Harvard Business School, say that many teams fail because of common barriers within organizations that are often neglected or not discussed.

The killing spiral of silence

Reducing employee silence, then, is a key concern for managers. Subrahmaniam Tangirala, assistant professor of management and organization, with co-author Rangaraj Ramanujam, Vanderbilt University, examined how the effects of individual-level variables such as professional pride, loyalty to the organization and individual perceptions of organizational fairness and supervisor status affected employee silence. They also looked at the effect of a group-level variable and the climate of fairness in the workplace.

The authors used data from a survey of front-line nurses in several large Midwestern hospitals. They chose nurses as their study group, because employee silence in a hospital context can have serious and even fatal consequences for patients, with as many as ninety-eight thousand Americans dying each year from preventable medical errors. Why would nurses, whose professional identity is bound to in-patient care, choose to stay silent even in a life-or-death situation?

The answer appears to be twofold, says Tangirala. People don't speak up because they fear retaliation against themselves, or because they are hesitant to point out the flaws of their peers.

Silence is the weapon of the passive aggressor. He or she is a petulant child choosing silence and non-cooperation to show his resentment or anger or disapproval.

When silence can carry its weight

Susan Scott in her book, *Fierce Conversations*, writes on *letting silence do the heavy lifting*. How do we do that? How can we allow silence to fill and carry on a better conversation?

> **There is a Zen saying, "It is the silence between the notes that makes music; it is the space between the bars that cage the tiger."**

Silence is better when we to allow people to think and assimilate. In my classes, if I were to ask a question and wait twenty seconds, a couple of answers will emerge. By simply waiting forty seconds or even a minute the number of answers increase by 40 percent. Silence allows the mind to think, and by not giving your mind enough time to think, any lesson is essentially a monologue.

We live in an open online world with everyone shouting his or her opinions out for the world to see. What happens when you have a person writing hate messages to you? Right now silence is your best ammunition. Refusing to hold a conversation with a person who does not talk with manners is not an escape attitude. It is a preference to avoid engaging in the dirty sludge of bad words and chaotic emotions.

Silence carries its weight in gold. It gives us time to reflect and actually allows the room to participate better. In the words of Susan Scott, "Silence encourages us to explore a more difficult peace."

Exactly what to say

1. Allow spaciousness in conversation—build silences into conversations so that people can reflect and answer.
2. In case you need time to think say, "I need a minute to reflect on what to say."
3. Do not use silence to escape a difficult situation.
4. Do not use silence to show disapproval in any relationship. (Unless it is one where you want to try and avoid the relationship.)

Conversation 16

The Art of Talk in the Digitally Distracted World

"Texting offers just the right amount of access, just the right amount of control. She is a modern Goldilocks: for her, texting puts people not too close, not too far, but at just the right distance. The world is now full of modern Goldilockses, people who take comfort in being in touch with a lot of people whom they also keep at bay."

Sherry Turkle,
Alone Together: Why We Expect More from Technology and Less from Each Other

We have a new soul mate. We take him or her along to every meeting, dinner, classroom, workplace, shopping and cricket match, even to the bathroom—yes! The intimacy that we show to this new soul mate, our mobile phones, is far more than any other object in the human race.

It is an irony to be writing about conversation in a digital world. We are always talking, aren't we? We may not be talking but texting, liking, posting, sharing, commenting, swiping, tweeting, buying, selling, browsing what your neighbors are buying, and every few minutes refreshing. A word that used to mean something new and fresh now reeks of a desperate attempt by the humankind to keep swiping at the screen, to see if they could somehow make their lives more refreshing, like the next post, like, comment, or mail that is going to cure them of this desperate living.

Today we live in the world of illusion. The illusion of relationships, a large number of friends, infinite choices, freedom, and our voices are actually heard. We have moved from strong relationship building to dating apps that give us an illusion of infinite choices.

In this distracted mind, we grow, build empires, work, marry, and raise children. The most important fact is that the digital world is here to stay. We cannot not have a world free from digital distraction, but we can try to build our lives and our conversations over the seduction of the sleek mobile phone.

Today we see employees sitting in an open office, specifically created to have a friendlier and collaborative work culture, wearing earphones, and working furiously on their laptops. They have converted the open floor into invisible private islands.

How does this digital world affect conversation?

> **The current world does not merely affect conversation; it has killed empathy, holding the knife over a bleeding generation that has no idea about reaching out to another human.**

Yes, the collective cry of social media is huge. The Chennai floods in 2015, the Kerala floods in 2018, the NEET exam, the Government policies are echoed by the voices of many. Yet single hands reaching out across the dining table to comfort, support, protect, or just share a laugh is decreasing.

It is easy to change your profile picture to show that you support a cause, rather than actually walk on the streets improving a situation. Research shows a shocking decrease in empathy in people, over the last few decades. Technology is noted to bean assault on empathy. We have learned that even a silent phone hinders conversations that matter.

In my classrooms, I have often found mobile phones act as a source of emotional and intellectual crutch that the students use.

The eye moves to the screen every time the class is asked to share, think, or talk. In times when the only intelligence was natural intelligence, the word meant a whole lot more than the numerical ability and information gathering. It meant reasoning, arguing, questioning, curiosity, sensitivity, awareness, and some humor. Our entire education system is confined to the first page of the search engine Google.

Some classrooms have a strict no device rule. Many of my classes do too. However, if the lesson itself is a rip off from the search engine, the class can be taught any subject, but they are only gathering information.

Imagine a classroom full of curious minds. Imagine the topic to be challenging, honest, and enthusiastic. Every student is involved in learning, understanding, and analyzing the concept. Asking questions that were never asked before. Ending the class with a few questions still ringing in their minds for them to contemplate as they leave the room...That will be a stimulating conversation. One that makes us think.

As these students join the workforce, they use the same technique in a meeting. Meetings are places where the collective mind creates something totally unheard of until then. The philosopher Heinrich von

Kleist calls this *the gradual completion of thoughts while speaking*. Von Kleist quotes the French proverb "appetite comes from eating" and observes that it is similar to "ideas come from speaking."

However, such conversations require time and space. The virtual world offers a lot of space and robs all our time. Having all the information in your palm has made your mind impatient. It cannot wait for people to think and answer. It does not wait while heavy decisions are being made.

The posts, messages, and texts are fine. It is the impact they have on actual relationships and the real conversations that matter.

The Art of Talking Today

Exactly what to say

1. Revisit the old table manners—learn how to have real-time conversations at dinner, meetings, and classrooms.
2. Keep distractions of the technological nature away, while having real conversations.
3. Have a face-to-face conversation for anything important. No employee wants to know that he has done a bad job or is being fired via phone or email.
4. Do not use the phone to avoid a conversation.

Conversation 17

Manager's Everyday Tough Talks

"A manager is a guide. He takes a group of people and says, 'With you I can make us a success; I can show you the way."

Arsene Wenger

What does your everyday life as a manager look like—playing referee to a team disagreement, agony aunt to an employee's off the record problems, being the quality auditor or sensitive mediator, policing the underperformer, mentoring the new recruit, or motivating and dealing with employee absenteeism, lateness, turnover, demands, and performance?

I am sure you can give me a longer list. Nevertheless, these everyday conversations can be potential pitfalls. Your regular workday is busy enough without involving employee tension and conflict.

Some issues are sensitive in nature. Sexual harassment in the workplace is one such issue. While company policy strictly spells out consequences of harassment, in reality it is difficult to pin down many discriminatory behaviors. Discriminatory banter, leering, and over friendliness can be denied and may not be witnessed. While it is essential to have an immediate talk with your employee in case of a complaint or even raise it to HR, such cases are not everyday battles.

Performance issues on the other hand are real-time everyday issues. Unmet sales targets, ineffective customer care responses, delays, and errors are all performance transgressions that require tough talks.

Every day tough talks

In one of my leadership coaching sessions, my participant was a meticulous person who would cross every 'T' and dot every 'I' but would often sacrifice the larger picture.

Such employees are an asset to the organization for their meticulous work. Unfortunately, neither do they see the distant future growth nor does their team develop. They also fall into the trap of making their perceptions into the gospel reality. Plato, 2400 years ago got it right in his dialogue Theaetetus. He defined 'knowledge' as "justified true beliefs." As a manager in a difficult situation,

> **Instead of trying to define reality for your team ask them "How do you know that is true?" Ask questions that break their stale rationalizations and make them dissect their opinion**

As a manager, there is no escaping the tough everyday conversations that you need to have. It can be decisions related to the culture of team, performance of the team, issues relating to absenteeism, turnover, salary, budget, projects, etc. They are not exactly listed out in your job description, but these issues take a majority of your time every week. It is in these everyday conversations that the rubber meets the road in any organization. What you say is less important than how you say it if you demonstrate respect and compassion, you are likely to receive a similar response. Remember all transitions are a gradual process and as a manager it is your responsibility to be aware of where your team member stands between letting go of the old and embracing the new.

In case of situations where the team has erred, your conversation should bring out the guilt of having made an error, not anger or a fear of losing the job. Ensure respect, social acceptance, and inclusive communication is present at all times.

The most important of all is perception. Ensure you use words to show that this is your view and invite a dialogue.

Exactly what to say

1. Ask questions that explore the situation and the problem rather than the outcome.
2. Instead of the 'what went wrong' questions, explore 'why the decision was taken' and then allow the person to work himself out of the problem.
3. Support and be patient while the changes happen. Encouraging conversations at this point is more important than solutions.

Conversation 18

Dealing the Blame Game

> *"Once I gave up the hunt for villains, I had little recourse but to take responsibility for my choices...Needless to say, this is far less satisfying than nailing villains. It also turned out to be more healing in the end."*
>
> ***Barbara Brown Taylor***

Raghavan manages a team of eleven technically strong people. He has a consistent problem of delayed deliveries. On probing for the reasons of the delays, Raghavan has replies like—"I can't help it, the team delayed," "Sid was supposed to provide data, but he was late," "The team did not update me on the progress," "I need better resources. My team does not understand the word responsibility."

We thrive in a very competitive workplace and we all want our jobs to be secure. In the name of a false job security, we might be sacrificing personal accountability. Deflecting blame always is not a healthy or responsible mechanism.

Yet we may find from time to time some team members, subordinates, managers, and even leaders pointing their fingers at others.

It is one thing to make excuses like, the internet was down or the traffic was too much or the rains were too heavy; but quite another to cast blame on a fellow employee.

The difficult part of the blame game

Dealing with the person who passes the blame like passing the torch at the Olympic Games is a skill on its own. It is difficult to the person receiving the blame and the organization itself.

Firstly, blame is a contagious game. When anyone casts aspersions against another person, he or she is starting a chain of other blames to surface. Slowly you will have an entire team pointing fingers in all directions. Trust and rapport flies through the roof and productivity dies. Such a situation in the long run will give rise to a blame culture.

It is imperative to understand at this point that the people who blame, especially in the workplace—are the ones who have had years of experience with success, in blaming others.

Maybe it worked for them in their childhood. Shouts and tears alike create the same experience and it has often worked for them. It is with this successful blamer that you have to tackle the situation.

> **The key to dealing with people who blame is to never be caught up in their justifications.**

1. Keep the focus on the problem at hand and the employee.
2. Listen to everything they have to say but don't allow them to throw the issues back at you.
3. Most importantly, look for personal accountability and talk firmly only from the single controlling factor—the employee.

Exactly what to say

Let us draft the conversation with Raghavan.

Manager: Hi Raghavan, I have asked this meeting to talk about the PAN project. You are aware that the delivery was delayed and it had to be significantly redone before passing it to the client. Please help me understand what went wrong?

Raghavan: I am glad you asked. The team initially told me they could do it. I trusted them. Later when the deadline had passed, they showed me areas where they were confused. In addition, throughout they just kept quiet.

Manager: Ok I hear you. So what steps did you take to monitor their progress?

Raghavan: Well, I asked them to escalate when needed. I keep my door and phone open at all times. I trusted them.

Manager: Let us talk on what we CAN control. What steps did YOU take?

Raghavan: I told you I trusted them. It's their fault.

Manager: Listen, I don't want to talk about your team. I want to talk about you. I want to know the exact role you played as the person-in-charge, in managing the project. What were your milestones? How many team meetings did you have? How was the progress mapped? When were the first delays?

(As a boss, you should never pass the blame or look for someone to censure to get yourself off the hook. As the boss, you hired and managed all the people who work under you, so, ultimately, the buck stops with you. After making Raghavan realize his areas of improvement, it is important to guide him through personal accountability, as it is your duty.)

Manager: So for the upcoming project, let us meet every Thursday to discuss the progress. Please ensure your team reports their progress every day to you.

(In addition, let employees know that it is ok to make mistakes as long as they have learned from them; it's the only real way they can work without fear and have the confidence and creativity to try new things.)

Conversation 19

Battle of Intentions and Influence

"It ain't what you don't know that gets you into trouble. It's what you know for sure that just ain't so."

Mark Twain

We live in a hawker's market. Everyone is selling us something. A simple search on Google. I begin typing how and I get around ten prompts from how to kiss to how to make a bomb. One weekend I decided to keep the internet world away and go to a family function. I was immediately advised about particular diets, hair care products, and shopping areas. One particular encounter was from a passionate gentleman who I was meeting for the first time. He spoke at length about a customized vegan diet that will suit me. He was a volunteer at the center advocating the diet.

Today if the fictitious genie did come and give me the power to read minds, I fear that I may find the same question in every mind around me:

In office,
How to get the boss to like my idea
How to get the client to accept the proposal
How to get the team to work faster
How to ace that interview
How to...

At home,
How to make my parents give me extra internet time
How to make my parents allow me to go for the tour
How to make my spouse...
How to make the maid clean better...

All our minds are working toward making someone else do something our way... As a result, conversations are misunderstood and people often complain, "I did not mean that!"

Statements like "I didn't mean it that way" or "I didn't mean to" go around a lot because of the misinterpretation of what is said. Dale Carnegie, author of *How to Make Friends and Influence*

People, said, "90 percent of all management problems are caused by miscommunication."

That does not negate the dodging tendency of the statement. Let's face it. If you did not mean what you said or what you did then who did? How is it possible to behave in ways that did not mean anything at all to you?

A few behaviors cannot be pardoned, like shouting because you are stressed or drunk. Cheating or embezzling from the company's accounts and calling it *borrowing*, even with good intentions, create misinterpretation.

> **Remember Plato's observation—wise men speak because they have something to say, while fools speak because they have to say something.**

In other words, think about the intent of your message before speaking, and when speaking, choose language that is precise, clear, and easily understood.

Fortunately, Plato lived at a time when people did not constantly wait to pounce on you with their ideas. Today it is a world where, everyone wants to bend your views, decisions, and loyalty.

Living in this world we tend to look at everything from our viewpoint alone and this is the real disconnect. Using the outdated principles of persuasion taught in colleges, we try to manipulate the other person to see our view and therein lies the disconnect. To truly make a difference and reach out in a conversation, you need to hear the other person's point of view.

Good intentions are difficult and dangerous

Most people, most of the time, aren't really motivated to do what you want them to do. They don't realize your need or feel your urgency. It may not even be their priority. A common scenario in many households is observed as follows -

Mom to son, "If you are free today, clean your room."

As she rushes to office, she only hears a grunt that she perceives as a yes. It should be no surprise that when she comes back home, the room is still messy.

Mom: "I told you to clean your room. You promised you would do it too. Why is the room still messy?"

Son: "Mom, you said *If you are free today, clean your room,* and I was busy with my friends the whole day playing cricket."

From the mother's point of view, the room needs to be cleaned. She is working and her son is free that day. Simple logic. To not make it seem like a demand or even a strict instruction, the mother tries to be polite. From her point of view, it is a priority. Unfortunately, the son does not feel this as a priority and finds a loophole in mom's polite conversation, to meet his needs.

Getting people to do what you want actually reduces your influence on them. They become vary of you.

Mark Goulsten, in his book *Real Influence: Persuade Without Pushing and Gain Without Giving In,* says, "Good intentions can steer good people the wrong way. When you feel committed to doing the right thing, you can easily give yourself too much benefit of the doubt and ignore what other people are trying to tell you."

Let us consider another conversation -

Raghavan has been a great team member in the organization for the last four years. He has a good reputation and a great relationship with his boss, Sahana.

A colleague from another team offers him a lateral move with exciting opportunities and Raghavan wants to shift teams. In his organization, such lateral moves are accepted as long as his current line manager approves. Raghavan decides to talk to his boss about the move. He has prepared his proposal and meets Sahana.

Raghavan: "Sahana, I appreciate you meeting me today. I want to discuss a new opportunity that has come in another team. I am extremely happy in my current role; however, I have been here for four years and want to explore the opportunity to learn another dimension of the business."

Sahana: "I hear you Raghavan. Please wait for a few days and we can revisit this conversation."

Raghavan: "Please hear me out. I will ensure that my team will not be affected by this change."

Sahana: "It is not that Raghavan. Please wait the few days. I will call you for a discussion myself."

Raghavan: "Try to understand Sahana..."

Sahana: "Raghavan, I will call you."

Raghavan walks out feeling resentment and anger. He feels cheated. "I have worked for four years, and my boss cannot even hear my argument."

However, Raghavan here is the one at fault. He was so focused on how he could convince Sahana that he never bothered to find out why she was asking him to wait.

Sahana knew of the upcoming organizational restructuring that is yet to be disclosed. She has asked for wider roles for Raghavan that includes a promotion. Unfortunately, she is yet to hear from her superiors and, therefore, cannot commit to Raghavan.

Good intentions everywhere, just not into the minds of people.

Exactly what to say

<u>Mom to son on cleaning the room</u>

Mom: "You have no school today. Please take the time to clean up your room."

Son: "ok"

Mom: "So can I expect a clean room by evening when I am back home?"

Son: "Yeah, I am going out to play cricket. I will be back in the afternoon. I'll clean it that time."

Mom: "Great. Do you need a reminder?"

Son: "No. I have set it on my mobile. I will clean it mom, don't worry."

<u>Raghavan to Sahana</u>

Raghavan: "Sahana, I appreciate you meeting me today. I want to discuss a new opportunity that has come in another team. I am extremely happy in my current role; however, I have been here for four years and I want to explore the opportunity to learn another dimension of the business."

Sahana: "I hear you Raghavan. Please wait for a few days and we can revisit this conversation."

Raghavan: "You have always supported me all these years. I just want to know why you are keeping me waiting."

Sahana: "Trust me Raghavan. Things will work in your favor but please let us discuss this in a few days."

Raghavan: "Right then, Sahana. I will speak with you again in a few days."

Conversation 20

Leadership Conversations

"Most leaders and employees do not know what their strengths are. When you ask them, they look at you with a blank stare, or they respond to you in terms of subject knowledge—which is the wrong answer."

Peter Drucker

Congratulations. You are a leader now. The hands that clap for you and the smiles that toast your success, will be depending on your guidance on Monday morning. It is a tough job and you have to do it.

The minute the leadership hat is bestowed upon them; many look toward more projects and higher revenue. The most important role as a leader is building a relationship with your team. Most good relationships are simply a long series of conversations. Leadership by its very essence is hence a conversation.

Although I hear managers say that their job is exciting, they say that they would be happy if it did not involve people's issues. At this point, I really want to elaborate on their job description.

In the words of Shawn Moon, in *Talent Unleashed: 3 Leadership Conversations to Ignite the Unlimited Potential in People*, "Leadership today requires many things, but one of the fundamental roles of a great leader is to see, recognize, and ultimately unleash the talents and strengths of others. The leaders need to create a bonding attraction for these people to the organizations for which they work, so that these talents and strengths are not undeveloped and then lost to others in today's rapidly changing work environment."

Conversations transform life by giving it a sense of mission. As Kenneth Blanchard says, "The key to successful leadership today is influence not authority."

> **The most reliable tool we use to influence others is communication. All influential leaders are great communicators. Not just in making great speeches but in engaging people.**

In the words of Person and Stieglitz, "The image of an ideal leader has swung from the benevolent dictator in the Industrial Age to the servant leader in recent years." Simply put great leaders engage and connect with people. The depth of the engagement defines the influence that they can have. The area of leadership and influence is very broad and to keep it focused on the difficult conversations that a leader needs to have, the conversations are broken down into four categories.

Interaction
Dispersal of information from the management and taking it to the employees is not enough and such information exchange is not called communication. This means leaders have to shun the one-sided **monologue** and embrace the vital and unpredictable **dialogue**.

The advancement of technology has made the channels of communication more interactive and collaborative.

Inclusion

We have moved out of the command and control leadership style toward inclusivity, which goes a long way in boosting the employee morale. Involving the team in every conversation creates ownership in the minds of people and this raises the level of emotional engagement that employees bring to the organization.

Immediate

These are the *time-specific* conversations that every leader needs to have with his team. It can be about a job well done or an improvement. It can be because of certain team conflicts or personal performance issues. It can be anything positive or negative, but the minute it reaches the boss, he or she will need to react immediately.

These conversations are as important as any other team conversations and the time factor plays an important role. As a leader, you need to be the first one to congratulate, reprimand, or encourage your team.

Intention

The purpose of communication is as important as the conversation itself. As an employee, being told that you have done a great job is good to hear. Being in the loop of every development in the organization is fine. However, the employee would also want to feel supported during the times when his or her morale is low. Leaders who bring in the—"I value you" kind of conversations in their team discussions tell people that they are important.

CONVERSATION 21

THE OUTLIERS—WHEN CONVERSATIONS ARE NOT ENOUGH

"When dealing with people, remember that you are not dealing with creatures of logic, but creatures of emotion."

Dale Carnegie

This is a serious and dangerous chapter. In all honesty, I am a tad bit scared to pen this one. But the conversation is far too important to be avoided and having come this far in dealing with difficult conversations, it is important to understand the outliers.

I have often asked myself throughout the book if a good conversation is enough. Will the world really be a better place if only people knew how to talk?

Will people who are depressed, suicidal, or criminal become normal and rational with conversations alone?

Most importantly, I want to write about what the scope of the book is, and to glimpse at what lies outside of its boundaries.

There are the regular garden varieties of difficult conversations. That is what this book has been about and with the help of the "Exactly What To Say" section; you can deal with most of those conversations on your own.

On the other hand, there are some seriously irrational people and dealing with such people may be high above your ability and the scope of this book.

The world outside is filled with people diagnosed with anxiety, Post-traumatic stress disorder (PTSD), depression, severe behavioral problems, addiction and even homicidal thinking. Nearly every newspaper daily covers news about irrational people.

It can be the highly intelligent teenager swallowing a whole bottle of pills, a cyber-stalker troubling a celebrity, family members killing each other, or even malicious customers.

While the defining boundaries of rational and irrational are a bit blurred, Mark Goulsten in his book, *Talking to Crazy* says irrational people:

- Can't see the world clearly
- Can say or think things that may not make sense.
- They can take decisions that aren't in their best interests
- They can become downright impossible when you guide them with reason.

When you know someone you love is going through turbulent times, will merely reaching out and having a happy chat suffice?

The chapter on irrational behavior is still the vanilla variety of people who can listen to rational. They were probably stressed, or unable to look at the situation from another angle.

What happens when the team member you feel is a negative person is actually battling the crippling side effects of some medication, is in the middle of a financial crisis, or is going through divorce or addiction?

What do you do when your team member is terrified of his or her own thoughts and is ready to give up? These are situations where friendship and empathy are important, but it is imperative that you scrape up enough courage to call for professional help.

Why is this conversation important?

This conversation chapter is particularly important to all my readers because, having understood how to transform difficult encounters into productive conversations you will be well on your way to forging great relationships.

As a result—many will approach you with their problems, and hence it is important to know when a good conversation helps and when to ask for professional help.

Not all emotional outbursts are a conversational glitch. Sometimes a person may be suffering from deep anger management issues. He or she may require counseling or even psychosocial rehabilitation. In the chapter dealing with the loquacious person, we spoke of people talking too much. One of the reasons for incessant talk might be a behavioral disorder.

There is a school of thought that those people with social disorders are more likely to blame others; it is also closely linked to bipolar disorder. If you manage such people, you may want to take specialist expert advice on how to handle this.

The virtuous silence can be passive aggression, an adjustment disorder, or a case of low self-esteem. While a few of these may not need professional help, a chat over coffee might not be the ideal solution either.

Most importantly, if you are a parent you will need to keep an eye out for your child's behavior. As a parent, your child's behavior is your responsibility.

However, this does not mean that you are now in charge. The "I say, you do" kind of dictatorial talk should have been abandoned long ago.

It is a relationship and although you are the adult, you cannot take unilateral decisions. Instead, you can listen, empathize, agree, and understand. Someday if you are lucky, your child will reach back to you for support, inspiration, and growth.

What you tell your child is less important than what you enable your child to tell you.

> **Here is my recommendation—call in reinforcements in case of serious problems.**

The Beginning!

I am honored that you have read this far and I am happy to share my ideas about the difficult conversations with you.

I have done my best to select the conversations that you will find most difficult, and approaches that are both powerful and doable.

But here is what I want to know.

Are there any other conversations you find difficult?

Are the strategies working for you?

I hope you will share them with me. It can be your success story or you may want to vent that the strategy backfired—I would love to hear from you both ways. I am on LinkedIn, Facebook, and you can reach me on my website, www.drlathavijaybaskar.com

I have also started a Facebook Group called "Handling

Difficult Conversations" to bring more people together and share productive ways to solve issues.

Just one more thing before you turn this page.

THANK YOU.

I began my journey as a Communications and Leadership coach and trainer, with the vision—words are the ideas on which change is built.

My burning desire is to make EVERY conversation effective.

By reading this book, and every time you motivate yourself to have a difficult conversation—you have made my vision come true.

Thank you so much!
~ Dr. Latha Vijaybaskar

Author Bio

As a professional and academic communication specialist, Dr. Latha Vijaybaskar works at the intersection between employee engagement and organizational communication. Trained and experienced in interpersonal, managerial, leadership, and corporate communications, she has worked with individuals and Organizations in real estate, IT, the financial sector, retail, and academia.

Latha is on a mission to create life-changing communication such that every time a person speaks or writes, they have the power to shape thinking and inspire action. As a coach, Latha works with both individuals and executive teams who have admitted to showing remarkable improvements in their engagement with peers and customers.

As visiting faculty at B-Schools in India, she teaches organizational behavior and business communications to the future managers and leaders. Academically, Latha's doctoral degree is in organizational communication with a research focus on the impact of internal corporate communication on employee engagement. She has three master's degrees: one in psychology, one in management, and an M.Phil. But first, – she is a bookworm. When she is not working, you can find her amidst her collection of books with her nose buried in the pages.

You can learn more about Latha and her programs at
www.drlathavijaybaskar.com

www.ingramcontent.com/pod-product-compliance
Lightning Source LLC
Chambersburg PA
CBHW030631220526
45463CB00004B/1489